Uppity Women
OF MEDIEVAL TIMES

Vicki León

CONARI PRESS
Berkeley, California

Conari Press books are distributed by Publishers Group West

Cover design: Claudia Smelser
Cover painting: Edmund Dulac
Interior design: Suzanne Albertson

ISBN: 1-57324-039-7

Library of Congress Cataloging-in-Publication Data

León, Vicki, 1942
    Uppity women of medieval times / Vicki León.
        p.   cm.
    Includes bibliographical references and index.
    ISBN 1-57324-039-7 (trade paper)
    1. Women—History—Middle Ages. 500-1650. 2. Women—Biography.
HQ1143.L46   1997   97-4483
305.4'09'02—dc21   CIP

Printed in the United States of America on recycled paper
10 9 8 7 6 5 4 3 2 1

Uppity Women
OF MEDIEVAL TIMES

To my uppity ancestor,
Adelicia Louvein,
discovered in the course of doing this book;
and to all the other
lion-hearted women of medieval times
whose unsung lives and antics
deserve a rousing new chorus.

UPPITY WOMEN OF MEDIEVAL TIMES

When Uppityhood Twas in Flower

AS SHAKESPEARE, A MEDIEVAL WRITER who had trouble spelling his own name, once said, "What's in a name? That which we call a rose by any other name would smell as sweet." Get real, Will: Instead of "Lady Macbeth," try answering to "what's-'er-name" or "Hey, wench!" and see how you would have liked it.

What with famines, plagues, marathon wars, and long church services with no central heating, the middle ages (470 A.D. to 1650 or so) were a trying 1200 years for everyone. Nevertheless, a dashing number of more-than-fair-damsels used their wits (and other weaponry from courage to guile and garden-variety impudence) to make *their* names around the world. Yes, the world. We tend to link "medieval" with Europe—but as you'll see, uppity women were busy blasting holes in the status quo on other continents, too.

The years from 500 to 1000 A.D., once labelled the Dark (as in "we don't know diddly about them") Ages, *were* dark—as in dirt-encrusted, soot-stained, blood-spattered, and plague-pocked. Organized religions were the major growth industry. Out of Islam, Christianity, and Buddhism came most of the educational and career opportunities for women. (Later, as the jobs and power got better, males tried to make it a boys-only clubhouse.)

Brainy females like English educator and convent-founder Hilda of Whitby and poet and passionate nature-lover Maysun of Syria role-modeled their way to fame in European and Islamic societies. In other parts of the world, Viking leader Aud the Deep-Minded colonized Iceland, announcing: "Hey! Big chunks of it are green!" Further south, powerful ladies like Zac-Kuk manipulated ruling sons and occasionally called the shots in supermacho Mayan territory. In Asia, any number of women romped to rulership; some, like astronomy-smitten Korean queen Sonduk, went the legal succession route; others, like Wu Zhao of China, chose to concubine, connive, murder, and Machiavelli her way to a fifty-year reign.

Starting about the year 800 A.D., a plague-free, 500-year warming trend hit the planet. Balmy nights being what they are, there was an orgasmic spurt in population. Medieval villages lacking sanitation became filthy cities, and, by 1300 A.D., another round of worldwide epidemics, notably the Great Dying (we call it Black Death), killed nearly half the folks in Europe, Asia, India, and the Islamic countries. To make matters worse, everyone began teeth-chattering through the next *five* centuries, euphemized as the Little Ice Age. By now religious modesty wasn't the issue: Women (and men) wore lots of clothes because it was *cold*, honey. Some wacko architect with a chilblains wish had also made stone castles popular; cathedral ceilings and frostbite weren't just for cathedrals anymore.

Ever since Christianity had declared, "The gym is closed" to the ancient Olympic Games in 395 A.D., enthusiasm for athletic pursuits had vanished. Depending on social class, women got their workouts by plowing, defending home and castle, riding into battles, running away from battles, and shivering. Even more unfortunate, the après-athletics custom of daily bathing got associated with paganism and disease. "Not gonna do it—wouldn't be prudent," asserted an ever-more-gamy populace. Picture a population of unwashed, overworked, ill-fed folks, all trying to get warm, and you've got the perfect environment for recurring waves of smallpox, bubonic plague, leprosy, and other diseases, followed by societal breakdowns and occasional cannibalism.

The female way with language came in handy in feudal days—"feud" being the operative word. Poring over the PMS-like accounts of the time, historians often marvel at the hair-trigger medieval temper, the violent behavior, and the physical abuse of those days. And the men were even worse! Thus humility (true Christian or tongue in cheek—they both worked) often seemed the better course of action for dames who wanted to keep their skulls intact. Whether performing unsung duty as washerwomen on the Crusades or rewriting a kingly husband's speech, the fair sex often said, "No, really—don't thank me—he did it all. . . ."

Life was especially hard on wives, even if you were lady of the manor. There were no hardware stores and no football games, so husbands tended to be underfoot a great deal. Therefore, when women caught wind of this Crusades idea, they wholeheartedly supported it. "Okay, you'll be gone what, a couple years? Make sure you rake the leaves and take out the garbage before you leave." Centuries of crusading led to three things: a big jump in the widow population, expanded employment abilities for women (somebody had to pick the locks on all those chastity belts), and a massive amount of deferred maintenance. Castles and villages alike resembled the "before" picture in a Sears ad.

People think of slavery as a phenomenon of ancient times, but it hadn't fallen out of fashion—unfree folks just had different names. Serfs, male and female, were like infrastructure: They came with the real estate. Although pricey, the best way to lose the "serfer girl" label was to become a nun—no wonder convents did a booming business. Highborn women, on the other hand, were business pawns, expected to make power marriages with other noble families, no matter how distant. As a result, star-quality queens like Nur Jahan of India and Eleanor of Aquitaine acted as cultural Johnny Appleseeds, transmitting inventions, foods, customs, languages, and institutions more profoundly (and sanely) than wars ever did.

If there had been any weather people around 1350, they might have said, "Expect clearing skies, with isolated patches of plague and famine, followed by the shiny bright splendor of the Renaissance, beginning in Italy and moving west to Britain by the sixteenth century." A high-energy age with a vivid interest in the humanities, the arts, and science, the Renaissance offered three centuries when women from Good Queen Bess (who made England debt-free) to Moll Cutpurse (whose Robin-hoodish activities redistributed the wealth) made their mark with renewed vigor.

It wasn't all sunshine. As if the world hadn't suffered enough with epidemics, there was that terrible day in 1385 when a Bavarian queen-to-be imported a fashion virus called "the hennin" into France. Women across Europe soon succumbed to this conehead-shaped fashion object, whose 3-foot steeples led to massive doorway remodels and even draftier castles. Despite the handicaps of hennin mania and non-stop pregnancies, women were eager to take on new endeavors.

A truly horrible new peril awaited, however, which traumatized all women—and in some places, exterminated them. From 1500 on, Europeans began to demonize female healers (and ultimately, almost any female), saying their powers came from the devil. Thus began 200-plus years of witch hunts, a church- and government-sponsored holocaust in which 100,000 women (by the most conservative estimates) were tortured, then burnt or ritually killed. The scapegoats tended to be, in the words of historian Anne Barstow, "uppity women, given to speaking out."

Lying low would have seemed to be a wise course. And many women did just that, for centuries. But others plunged into Renaissance enterprises on a variety of continents. Vixen vagabonds set out to explore (and sometimes, to exploit) like their male counterparts. For instance, Inés de Suárez, a Spanish adventurer who led the expedition of Pedro "I don't need to stop and ask directions!" Valdivia out of the desert and to a decent city-founding site. Or Maggie de la Roque, whose plucky survival in the wilderness of early Canada sans malls or decaf *lattes* won her a bio written by a queen. And who can forget Nzinga Mbande, warrior ruler of Angola, who got rid of Portuguese colonizers—on occasion, by eating them.

During this rambunctious age, women took up anatomy, astronomy, and religious activism. Career seekers became blacksmiths and butchers, printers and philanthropists, wool merchants and pull-the-wool scam artists. Whatever their social class, wherever their home town, they had a chin-up attitude, epitomized by Artemisia Gentileschi. An Italian painter on the rise, her career was brutally interrupted by rape. At the trial, Artemisia as witness underwent months of thumbscrew torture (the medieval idea of a lie detector). She rose above that additional brutality, got a conviction, and went on to say, "As long as I live, I will have control over my being." Artie wreaked the very best revenge on her attacker—by going on to greatness, in her work and as a person.

Amid the credulous, sometimes glorious, sometimes dangerous, often uncomfortable chaos of medieval times, countless women rose to the occasion—and to fame or notoriety—just as they had done and would continue to do throughout history. No matter how dark the age or how crummy the weather, there were a darned sight more female names on hand than we've heard about to date—gals with derring-do, who did and dared and said, "Righteously stink though it may, this is my planet, too. Oh, and Will—make sure you spell *my* name right!"

Making Hay in the Middle Ages

Fya upper Bach

Shades of Rosy the Riveter—a woman with the delightful name of Fya upper Bach (I guess the upper Bachs wanted to distance themselves from those trashy lower Bachs) took advantage of the career opportunities in blacksmithing—and did it six centuries before American women were exhorted to get into heavy metal for the World War II war effort. Fya, who lived and made horseshoes in

14th-century females: into heavy metal

Germany, first became an independent mastersmith known as the "smithy of Siberg." Later she moved her anvil into the city of Cologne. Besides an aptitude for pounding red-hot iron, Fya had leadership qualities. Twice in her thirty-year career she held office in the blacksmiths' guild. Ms. upper Bach was no fluke, either: legal and guild records from medieval Germany list other female blacksmiths, coppersmiths, tinsmiths, and pewterers. Some of these redoubtable women gained entry into the guild through "widow's rights"; others, however, made it on sheer mettle and muscle.

Margery Russell

Suddenly short one husband around 1300 A.D., surprised widow Margery Russell gamely stepped up to the plate as head of her late lamented's import-export business in Coventry, England. Things were going pretty well until one of her ships, laden with goods worth more than 800 English pounds, got knocked off en route. It had to be Spanish pirates—the infamous downside of doing business in that time and place. Margery marched into court, demanding letters of marque against Santander, Spain, the pirates' port of origin. (Letters of marque were documents from the English king that licensed a victim of high-seas robbery to seize Spanish-owned cargo—that is, goods belonging to any Spaniard, not necessarily the guilty parties—from English ports as compensation.) After Mrs. Russell got her letters, she got dibs on two Spanish ships, whose nicely bulging holds turned out to represent substantially more than the value of what the pirates took.

This tactic, standard operating procedure among merchants of her time, provoked a roar of legal anguish from the Spaniards—ample proof that even with a late-inning start, this game dame knew how to play business hardball.

Alison La Jourdain

t's hard to believe of gay Paree, but, in 1415 at least, a gal could get into beaucoup hot water over a search for a stylish dress and maybe a little independence. The clothes-hound in question was Alison la Jourdain, a young married woman from Senlis who'd gradually come to see that the wedded state didn't suit her. Before plunging into singlehood, however, she prudently took up a trade: hatmaking. After her divorce, she also got into the weavers' guild and worked in the cloth trade, doing well enough to hire apprentices. As a mark of her success, she bought a good house (with room for twelve boarders as a sideline) with her own money.

So one day, she was walking around Paris, maybe a little overstated in a belted ensemble with fur trim but minding her own business, when a constable ran her in for breaking the sumptuary laws. (Parisian law in Alison's day was enough to make Yves St. Laurent run for the smelling salts: It forbid female finery—especially for nonnobles—to be too fine. Sumptuary laws existed elsewhere in Europe, too. In some locales, a woman faced the ultimate horror: Her best clothes and jewels were owned by her husband, which he had the right to sell or rent to others! In a more enlightened age, that would be grounds for divorce right there.)

After an official reprimand for her apparel, Alison was told she would be evicted from her house as punishment. And thus began a confusing, rancorous court case between citizen Alison and the Big Brother fashion cops of Paris.

The attorney for the city, determined to show the connection between haute couture and sexual excess, painted Alison as a loose woman who cheated on her ex-hubby with a priest—and, if that weren't disgraceful enough, with an Italian. A witness from Alison's guild asserted that Jourdain's fancy digs might serve as a weaving establishment by day, but when the lights go down low—look out: Madam Jourdain was running a bawdy house out of her living room. Other witnesses claimed Alison acted as a pimp for her two sisters; while still others just as strenuously testified that since La Jourdain didn't take any money, this wasn't pimping but just "being good company."

Did the lavishly furred, possibly scarlet Ms. A beat the rap and keep her house? Did the evil bureacracy succeed in pillorying her for being chic? Or was Alison's case really about zoning? (You see, if she were running a twenty-four-hour weaving operation out of her home, no Parisian would object to a dozen looms thundering away next door. But even a part-time house of ill repute in a commercial zone was out of the question. Because then Alison would have an unfair advantage over the other cathouses in town: heavy foot traffic. So very French, isn't it, to think of apprentices torn between grabbing a quick bite for supper—or a quickie at supper?!)

Just like those bittersweet French films, we (and Alison) are left hanging. In classic bureaucratic fashion, the court agreed only "to study the matter a bit further."

Katharina Johans & Alewives

Whether you called them typelers, gannokers, hostelers, tapsters, or just plain alewives, women dominated the bed-and-brew field in medieval times. From making it to selling it, beer was a female-dominated occupation, and long had been.

Brewmasters like Lisebette de Hond, a prosperous citizen of Ghent, Belgium, appear often in the municipal records. This lady came from a beer-making dynasty, married a brewster, made beer herself after he died, trained workers, and later rented out her brewery when she wanted to sit back and sip in the late 1300s.

Another bold brewster and innkeeper named Katharina Johans juggled a variety of jobs. In the Germany of her day, inns served as much more than places for food, drink, and lodging. Innkeepers acted as information centers and mediators, provided entertainment and medical services, arranged credit for their customers, and even served as pawnbrokers. Obviously that system broke down on occasion. Katharina had to get ugly with one of her regulars, writing him nasty letters to pay up his bar tab. Although this plucky alewife was within her rights, Mr. Accounts Way Overdue was a local figure and took the matter to the Erfurt city council—whereupon poor Katherina had to apologize to him at a council meeting. (It's not recorded when—or whether—she got her money.)

Vikings loved ale as much as the English; women as well as men were judged on their ability to down huge quantities of the stuff. English alewives were often immortalized in print and portrait. During the time of Henry VIII, a pub at Leatherhead run by Eleanor Rummynge became the favorite watering place for John Skeleton, poet laureate of England and Henry's first tutor. A thirsty man with a cruelly witty pen, John caricatured the owner's unforgettable mug and wrote a ditty about her, called "The Tunning of Eleanor Rummynge."

Incidentally, it was in Eleanor's time that the beer versus ale controversy began. While monkeying around with new brewing technology in their monasteries, European monks had discovered that adding a plant called "hops" to ale balanced the sweetness of the drink; even more important, the hops kept the beer from spoiling so quickly. Before long, Eleanor could pull her customers a draft of beer or ale. Ale, however, remained the traditionally English drink of choice. And Eleanor's rated among the best. As the often-quoted line from poet Skeleton's ditty said, "When Skeleton wore the laurel crown, my ale beat the alewives down."

Aedelfleda

Around 990, the flying fingers of English needlewoman Aedelfleda completed a huge tapestry depicting her husband's noble deeds in life and his death at the Battle of Malden. Aedelfleda presented it to the abbey church at Ely as a gift. Her handiwork (probably an embroidery rather than a woven tapestry) no longer exists—but many think her creation inspired the making of the famous 231-foot-long Bayeux Tapestry, a female team-effort needlework of wool on linen, whose "cartoon panel" format depicts two historical events: the Battle of Hastings and Halley's Comet. Long after Aedelfleda's 20/20 vision and way with a thimble were no more, the head of the abbey at Ely awarded her granddaughter an entire village as a site where she and her most talented textile artists could continue their work—a commitment to an artistic tradition begun by this talented Sussex woman.

Chiyome

A shrewd Japanese widow who worked all the angles, Chiyome knew it's better to be at the top of a pyramid scheme than scuffling on the ground floor. With that principle in mind, around 1560 she started her own rent-a-ninja business, training girls to become *kunoichi* or "deadly flowers," as they were called.

Before ninjas mutated into the sappy cartoon turtles and Halloween costumes they are today, they worked as spies during most of Japan's thousand-year medieval period. In this class-conscious society, samurai warlords used ninjas to do their dirty work: spread subversion, discover enemy plans, or knock off unwanted political figures or other samurais. Popular as they were as a labor force, ninjas got about as much prestige and pay as burger-flippers in a fast-food chain. Thinking "volume business," Chiyome saw it would make more economic sense to train ninjas rather than be one; as the not-so-bereaved spouse of a warlord, her home-alone situation gave her the necessary privacy to set up a clandestine school.

Traditionally, ninjahood got passed down from one generation to another within ninja families, most of whom lived in remote villages in the Iga and Koga districts. Our female Fagin, however, had the clever idea of taking in the throwaway kids of her time—orphans, runaways, and the like. How sweet, the neighbors thought, failing to notice the whizzing sound of those throwing-blade stars.

In her school, Chiyome's trainees learned to use martial arts, knives, swords, spears, and an axe-spear combo called the halberd. Deadly flowers also had to improvise, James Bondlike, turning anything into a killing tool. Hairpins got dipped in poison. A lady's fan got sharpened to a razor point. Her ninjas carried an array of projectiles, steel claws, blinding powders, and other cool stuff, lashed to their waists with sashes called *obis*—a nine-foot-long piece of cloth that could double as climbing gear and field bandage.

Most of the girls looked forward to wearing the "cloak of darkness" black ninja garb (so slimming!); sometimes, however, they used street clothes. Boss Chiyome often got assignments that called for womanly wiles—for which her deadly flowers had to drag out the kimono with the plunging neckline.

Besides weapons training, the young and the invisible spent countless hours tree-climbing, hiding underwater, and learning to dislocate their joints for easier escape from small places or from being tied up. No matter how slick they got, however, there was one situation they were highly unlikely to get out of—their bondage to the redoubtable Madame Chiyome.

Margaretha Prüss

"**I**nk turns me on" could have been the motto of Margaretha Prüss, a stick-to-it craftswoman from Strasbourg, Germany. In the mid-1500s, she was active in the printing industry, which had just gotten off the ground a hundred years prior, thanks to the German invention of movable type. Documents indicate that Margaretha broke into the ink-on-paper game via matrimony. Over the years, she married and buried three different printers, ultimately running the presses herself. What did Prüss print? Probably books and pamphlets. In her day, printers were also publishers, selling as well as printing their literary output. Censorship by city government and the church was alive and well, however, in Europe. Religious and political materials considered "too provocative" got confiscated; second offenders went to jail. The church itself could have been one of Margaretha's best customers. For years, religious officials had raised money by selling indulgences, a document that let you off the hook for a sin by paying a fee; now "fill-in-the-blank" indulgences could be generated in a flash. Printer Prüss and other female printing pioneers probably grinned all the way to the bank.

Liutbirg

In the ninth century, folks called weaving maven Liutbirg of Germany "a miracle worker"—and meant it in every sense of the word. Clothmaking was the industry to watch in Europe; after centuries of feudal no-growth, a retail renaissance was turning fortress-cities into urban centers. Most clothmaking, finishing, and dyeing was done in women's workshops, such as the good-sized one run by

Liutbirg, a humble Saxon servant of German Countess Gisla and son. These two knew an overachiever when they saw one. After honeyed words from her employers, loyal Liutbirg took on more chores: nursing the sick, administering the affairs of the palace, even running a swing-shift school for girls to teach them weaving, spinning, needlework, reading, psalm-singing, and cloth dyeing. At retirement, instead of asking for a putting green or entertainment center in her unplush quarters, Liutbirg requested a tiny prayer cell and a coal furnace, so she could continue to worship God, dye cloth, and teach the craft. Is it any wonder this Saxon perpetual motion machine got tapped for sainthood down the line?

Anna Weylandin

The career of a fraulein named Anna Weylandin illustrates one of history's fascinating lessons—the perennial desire of governments to over-regulate versus the equally fervid goal of citizens to wiggle around them. Anna, who lived in sixteenth-century Strasbourg, Germany, must have been one of that city's most ingenious sidesteppers of the law. The main clue? Her nickname—Lumpenweiblin or "rascal woman."

After getting a city permit to sell imported herring, wily Anna immediately baited and switched with dried cod, then engaged in illegal price cutting and other fishy maneuvers. Next she got into the candle business and was soon breaking various of the tediously complex beeswax ordinances and child labor laws. Strasbourg laws may have been ridiculous, but the punishments sure would have smarted: The council threatened to pinch Anna with a pair of glowing tongs and toss her into the water. (No record exists of her actually being punished in any way, however.)

Six years later, the council caught her—well, almost caught her—selling bantamweight candles. Lumpy refused to answer questions, sending in her husband, whose abilities at dodging and wiggling weren't bad, either. His antics dragged the matter out until the whole thing resembled the O. J. Simpson trial. The exasperated council finally forbid Anna to sell any and all candles and went home—exhausted but sure they'd stuck a finger in the regulations dike.

After the candle fiasco, Rascal Woman jumped to Dutch cheese, selling it illegally until the council caught on, threatened banishment, and slammed Anna with a lifetime ban against selling anything. Anything whatsoever. Without a scam to call her own, Strasbourg's favorite scalawag disappeared from the archives of the city council. (My guess is, researchers will someday find, amid the records of some other hapless city council, the meter-long rap sheet of a rogue female fishmonger/candlescammer/cheese-schlepper.)

Eva Giffard

In the middle of the thirteenth century, the port town of Waterford, Ireland, was shamrock green, covered with sheep, and a terrible place to make a living. A local weaver and wool saleswoman, Eva Giffard couldn't seem to get ahead, what with price hikes and all. Then it came to her—why not cut out the middleperson in the sheep racket? Accordingly, she identified a particularly fluffy group of animals and paid them a visit one night. In the heat of the moment, Eva may have forgotten her shears. On the other hand, maybe she wanted to leave the impression of an alien fact-finding tour. At any rate, Ms. Giffard rolled up her sleeves and ripped the wool right off the backs of twenty dazed sheep with her bare hands. Someone bleated, however. Eva was busted before she even got to page two of her business plan. Brought before a judge, Eva spun an excellent yarn and was almost set free, when an alert official thought to check her priors. Holy Saint Bridget! Turns out this wasn't the first time the law-abiding citizens—and sheep—of Waterford had been fleeced by this feminine bit of blarney. Make that a ewe-turn for Eva.

Esther Quira

urkish harem life being pretty monotonous, the women within loved to shop. Naturally, everything had to be delivered. In this way, Esther Quira, a young Jewish widow who'd become a vendor of luxury fabrics, perfume, and jewelry out of financial necessity, got to be friends with Baffa, the sultana and marital favorite of Sultan Murad Three. Multitalented Esther eventually became chief lady's maid, doing everything from helping at childbirth to acting as business agent, personal courier, and shopping go-between for harem residents. After reportedly saving the life of a young male heir who'd come down with smallpox, Esther's stock with the sultana really went sky-high. In 1539, she won the first of many special perks and incentives—tax-free status for life for her and her descendants.

For four decades, Esther mixed it up with the Moslem bigwigs of Constantinople, making money and learning the intrigue game. In 1584, she did a little light spying and translating in a delicate political matter between Catherine de' Medici and Sultana Baffa. In gratitude, the sultana gave Esther another gift—the right to start her very own lottery in Venice.

Now the faucet of royal favor was wide open; perks and honors for our busy widow flowed nonstop. As a peddler of influence instead of high-priced knick-knacks, Esther won a reputation as the woman with court clout. Quira used her money in good ways. She subsidized Hebrew scholars and book publication; and, after a devastating fire that left the Jewish quarter in cinders, this generous-hearted woman helped rebuild it—and fed the poor at her table too. Besides her influence in the Constantinople community and elsewhere, Esther may have introduced Gracia Mendes, Europe's most celebrated and wealthy Jewish refugee, into Turkish court society.

Human careers often resemble the law of gravity. In Esther's case, what went up, came down with a splat when she was in her seventies. As the next sultan came to power, a military faction, angry over their inability to bribe the longtime power broker, led a mob straight to her door. After killing Esther, they used her body parts to mark the doors of people who had gotten in on her gravy train. Among those slaughtered in the melee were two of Esther's sons. In the dustup, Quira's by-now fabulous wealth got confiscated by the Turkish government. Twenty years later, however, the privileges she had been awarded by the prior administration were once again bestowed on her grandchildren. Quira's fame kept its golden gleam, too; her surname Quira (the Turkish word for "Ester") became a generic noun. From the sixteenth century on, other inter-harem sales reps of note were called "kira" after Esther.

Anna Maria von Schurmann

What would you call a woman who learned a dozen languages, graduated with a law degree from Utrecht University, studied medicine, taught philosophy, wrote books, and in her spare time was a sculptor and painter of note? Unmarriageable. At least, that's what Anna Maria von Schurmann's mother thought. She wanted Anna to stick to needlework like normal upper-class girls born in 1607 did. Despite mom's angst, her Renaissance daughter eventually had the world knocking on her Dutch doors. Celebrity eggheads like Descartes exchanged ideas with Anna Maria. Besides scholarly works like her Ethiopian grammar, she wrote well-received books on gender-neutral intelligence and medicine. This striking brunette was dazzlingly multifaceted: In fact, one of her talents was engraving on glass with a diamond. Another was painting portraits with big price tags. In her late fifties, Anna embraced Labadism, a utopian religious community whose Quakerlike beliefs attracted a lot of flak in seventeenth-century Europe. That didn't matter an iota to Anna: She spent her last florins helping the poor and spreading the spiritual ideas of Labadism—an iconoclast to the last.

Isabella Andreini

So what if England's own Queen Elizabeth dug the theater—actresses were sluts, thundered the English, the Spanish, and the pope. Therefore, stage roles—male and female—went to men. Among those who failed to pay attention to these pomposities was Italian Isabella Andreini. A fine actress and musician, she wrote several plays, published poetry, and was elected to membership in the intellectual academy at Mantua. All this and respect, too: Isabella's accomplishments made her community proud enough to issue several medals of her head—an accolade usually given only to royalty. Backstage, Mrs. Andreini found time to birth seven children, who grew up untraumatized by their early involvement in Gelosi, the family's commedia dell'arte company, which toured Italy and France. At least one son started his own troupe in the 1600s. It was hard to top Isabella creatively, but daughter-in-law Virginia Andreini tried. She sang in her husband's productions, and in 1608 created the title role of *Arianna* in Monteverdi's opera.

Lavinia Fontana

Creative women have often lamented that they lack a key ingredient possessed by most successful male artists: a wife. Bravo to painter Lavinia Fontana, who negotiated just that—and a lot more, back in Bologna, Italy, in the mid-1500s.

Her husband Gian Paolo Zappi, a painter with more money than talent, had studied with Lavina's father, Prospero, before popping the question to the popular Miss Fontana. After marriage, however, Zappi was content to be Mr. Mom. Before they tied the knot, the two had worked out an arrangement highly unusual for the times: Zappi would raise their brood, confining his own modest abilities to filling in some of the backgrounds on Lavinia's work and making the occasional frame, while Lavinia supported the family with her art. (Zappi might not have consented so readily had he known that the offspring tally would hit eleven!)

A groundbreaking female in a number of ways, Lavinia broke through the artistic "glass ceiling," which often confined even the most talented women painters to smaller works, miniatures, and portraits. Fontana trailblazed the way by winning bids for big public art projects, such as church altarpieces. Prior to the 1570s, women were rarely entrusted with large-scale commissions, where the prestige and the generous paydays lay. She got top nugget for her work. Payment for her very first church altarpiece commission, for instance, amounted to 1,000 ducats—a huge amount of change in her day.

At age thirty-seven, already famous throughout Italy, Lavinia received her first big religious painting commission—an offer to do the altar at El Escorial, the vast and gloomy royal palace high in the mountains behind Madrid. Her *Holy Family* was a hit with the Spanish royals.

Hundreds of paintings and a decade later, another honor—court painter to the pope. Pope Clement VIII asked her to move to Rome, there to carry out further church commissions. She, Zappi, and the kids moved to the Eternal City, settled in, and Lavinia completed everything from mythological and historical paintings to a massive and controversial altarpiece, some twenty feet high.

Although she received criticism from time to time about some of her creations, life was basically good: People admired her; she was elected to the Roman Academy; she even started a nice collection of antiques. But into each life, some paint must spatter. For Lavinia, it was family tragedy. Her youngest daughter, Leodamia, showed a lot of promise as a painter—a potential that was never met. She died at age sixteen. Indeed, eight of Lavinia and Zappi's eleven children died young—an unkind statistic that speaks volumes about child mortality rates in medieval times, even among the well-to-do.

In 1611, a medal was struck in Lavinia's honor for her artistic achievements (over 135 of her works still exist). Fontana herself made it to age sixty-two, full of years and honored by Rome and Bologna alike.

Juliana

The English have always been mad for gardening—and mad for gardeners like Juliana. In the fourteenth century, at the celebrated cathedral near Cambridge, the bishop of Ely hired this green thumb gal as head gardener for his manor at Little Downham. Socially, Juliana may have been near the bottom of the food chain, but she was an entrepreneur who hired and oversaw a gang of village temps. At specified times of year, she and her compost corps planted and harvested everything from peas and leeks to all manner of fruit and nuts. This soil-amending sister and her muddy troops must have had elbow grease that wouldn't quit. After

she left the bishop's employ, later gardeners tried to make a new garden in the obdurate soil—and actually broke their shovels trying. Judging by local court records, Juliana had more going for her than just a way with seeds and slug bait. Her earnings allowed her to lease several meadows and a fishery and make several backdoor real estate deals—in the process becoming a slightly shady property owner herself.

Izumo no Okuni

In the fourth and fifth centuries around the Mediterranean, a musical theater and dance form called "pantomime" shot to the top of the charts. Eleven centuries later, in the Far East, a similar evolution in entertainment took place—spearheaded by a Japanese woman named Okuni. A dancer and religious drama performer, Okuni got involved in a benefit gig to rebuild a famous shrine and ended up touring with a company to raise money. On the road, she connected with a well-known comic, shared her ideas of melding mime and religious drama with him, and came up with Kabuki, the most popular genre of Japanese theatre for the past 400 years. Not long after that, Okuni teamed up with a samurai who added his knowledge of classical drama to her inventive idea.

This dancer-choreographer also started the Kabuki tradition of males playing female roles, and vice versa. Oh, how that woman could swash a buckle! Her adoring public and the Japanese royals loved her trademark attire—a black priest's robe and a couple of swords in her belt. Although Kabuki is still wowing audiences in Japan, its founder Okuni wouldn't even be able to get on stage nowadays—male actors now play all the roles.

Sofonisba Anguissola

The ghastly life of Vincent van Gogh, coupled with his formidable painting, has made popular the specious notion that "Great art requires great suffering." Hah, as Italy's Sofonisba Anguissola might have said. A formidable painter in an era when celebrated women artists were as rare as dancing dogs, Sofonisba won an international reputation, glowing reviews, and huge fees—while enjoying a close-knit family, two adoring husbands, travel, and many royal perks during her ninety-plus years.

Okay, she did go blind when she hit her eighties; nevertheless, famous painters like Antony Van Dyck were still knocking on her door, asking for quotes. The only not-so-great thing about Sofonisba's life, in fact, is its near-invisibility in history books. It's not like she didn't leave a legacy: Over a hundred works signed or attributed to her grace museums and homes throughout the world; and in 1995 she was the focus of an exhibition and symposium at the National Museum of Women in the Arts in Washington, D.C.

Who was this extraordinary artist of Cremona? Born in 1532, Sofie was one of seven children named for famous figures of mythology or Roman history. (Daddy was very big on the classics.) After studying Latin, music, and painting, all six girls became artists. Sofonisba and Lucia (who died young) were considered the most talented. After studying with two professional portraitists, Sofonisba had enough training to teach three of her sisters. Sofie's proud daddy continued to help, even writing to a now-elderly Michelangelo about her talent. His overture started a flurry of "learn to draw by mail" correspondence: Mike sent drawings, then Sofie copied them and returned them to him for critiquing.

Sofonisba matured quickly as an artist. At twenty-seven, she nabbed her first lucrative royal commission; she was hired by King Philip of Spain as court painter. There she remained for a number of years. Besides paying her a fabled amount, they sent her father a royal pension of 800 lira a year. At the Madrid court, she met and fell in love with a Sicilian lord named Fabrizio de Moncada. Closet romantics, her royal employers footed the bill for the wedding and gave Sofie a juicy dowry—even though the couple moved back to Palermo, Italy.

Four years later, her husband died. King Philip, still without a court painter, asked the widow Anguissola for a return engagement. While on a ship back to Spain, however, the painter got entangled romantically with the ship's captain. In Genoa, she and Captain Orazio married, dividing their time between Italy and Sicily after that.

One of Sofie's most-painted subjects was her own face. Her fame eventually reached such a *People* magazine–style level throughout Europe that clients clamored for her self-portraits. As one fan wrote, "There is nothing I desire more than an image of the artist herself, so that in a single work I can exhibit two marvels, one the work, the other the artist."

Through her art, Sofonisba punctured those pretensions. She made a practice of dressing soberly, a no-frills approach that emphasized her brain rather than her looks. As historian Mary Garrard pointed out, Sofonisba's family portraits—especially the picture of her three sisters, portrayed playing chess, a potent symbol of intellectual activity—give a low-key but unmistakable look at the patriarchal hypocrisy of her times. Although most of her Spanish output got destroyed in a fire, many of Sofonisba's self-portraits exist—a fascinating study, showing a consummately clear-eyed maiden who grew into a grand, no-flies-on-me old woman.

Sabina von Steinbach

Sometimes an artisan gal had to strike while the iron was hot—or before the corpse got cold. Around 1300, when a master sculptor died in mid-cathedral, Sabina von Steinbach of Strasbourg leaped into action. A stone mason, sculptor, and self-promoter, she supposedly won the contract and completed the job, finishing the statues that still adorn Strasbourg Cathedral. A scroll in the hands of the statue of Saint John says in Latin: "Thanks to the holy piety of this woman, Sabina, who has given me form from this hard stone." After passing along the story of this

save-the-day female hard hat for centuries, historians now think that the Sabina referred to in the inscription was the donor, not the creator. Okay. So now we have two Sabinas: a philanthropist who paid for the statues and a working-stiff mason (her name's in the church records) who contributed just as much to the cathedral through her own gut-straining, backbreaking labor. I say: give 'em both a round of applause.

Axes to Grind,
Places to Pillage

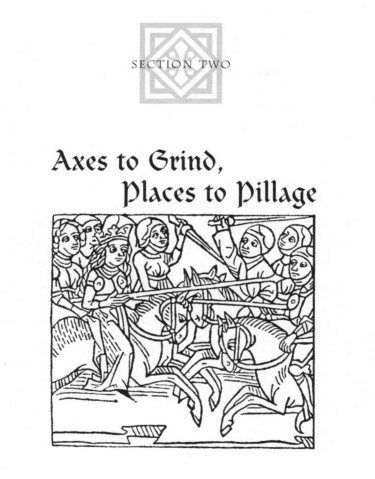

Wu Zhao

Becoming a grade-A concubine in seventh-century China was tougher than getting a black belt. Oh well, nowhere to go but up, thought Wu Zhao, at fourteen an entry-level mistress, one among the multitudes of concubines in Emperor T'ai Tsung's court. Favored with assassination skills as great as her looks, this fortunate cookie rapidly parleyed her rock-bottom status into much more.

First she caught the attention of the emperor's son Kao Tsung—an excellent move, because in a couple of years old T'ai Tsung died, which meant that his concubines got a one-way ticket into the convent. Not our Wu, however, who now had her black belt in eroticism. Further accolades followed, after she bore a son to new Emperor Kao. By the time Wu Zhao reached thirty, she'd edged out the number one concubine and was gaining on the empress herself.

Wu gave a luster to the expression "shameless opportunist" that it hasn't quite had ever since. Not only did she plug her accomplishment of having given the emperor an heir—she tirelessly pointed out how the empress hadn't. The empress and ex–number one concubine got so furious that they conspired together, a crime which made it a snap for Wu Zhao to get them jailed and quietly killed. With some judicious greasing of palms, Wu made empress by her thirty-first birthday. She celebrated by ordering the first of countless "disappearances," which came to include all concubines, argumentative family members, and high-ranking staff who showed signs of disagreeing with her.

In 660, she had another stroke of luck: Her somewhat dim but very doting husband, Kao, caught polio. Wu Zhao vaulted onto the imperial big chair, delighted to take over the war with Korea. Ordering an invasion by sea, she soon annexed the place to China. Merciless as she sounds, Wu knew how to rule. Her initial severity gave China decades of peace. She carried out various crowd-pleasing actions: improved government, new hospitals and health care for the mentally ill, new buildings in the capital, and that old favorite, lower taxes.

But exemplary behavior just wasn't Wu's style. After her husband died in 684, she took a cosmetics peddler as a lover. Despite her help, the guy just couldn't cut it as an abbot or a military commander. In the end, she lost patience and went back to the old maxim she'd lived by for so long: If they don't work out, shanghai 'em.

She tried again with the Chang brothers, who may have both been her intimates. Then again, maybe not: Wu was pushing seventy-one. In any event, this pair schemed to succeed her—which triggered the only coup Empress Zhao ever saw in her fifty years of rule. Ironically, the coup-meisters had the Changs murdered and put Wu's son (whom she'd also nudged out of the way in 690) on the throne.

Why fight it, our black belt thought. The most formidable female China would ever see in the top spot retired, played with her grandkids, and died in bed a few months later at her summer palace. Her grandson took advantage of Wu Zhao's legacy of tranquility and made his reign the apogee of T'ang art, poetry, and culture.

Olga & Tamara

Quick, name a couple of women who had a big impact on early Russian history. (Hint: Dr. Zhivago's sweetheart Lara, Catherine the Great, and Anna Karenina are *not* the right answers.) Although leadership of that ungainly chunk of terrain between Europe and China has seemed monotonously male over the millenia, Olga and Tamara were two bright spots—both with important parts to play in bringing Christianity to Mother Russia, as it turns out.

Around 945, a royal Russian dynamo named Olga was having a dickens of a time. Barbarians had just killed her hubby King Igor. As new ruler, she methodically went after the various rebel groups, wiping them out in ingenious ways designed to put the fear of Olga into the rest. The first batch, she buried alive; the second, she had boiled in their baths. After that, she and her army relied on the time-honored swords and sieges to bring everyone into line. When the smoke had cleared, people were pretty much ready to let Olga reign. And in 955, she did just that, introducing the Greek Orthodox form of Christianity to all of Russia (and you'd better believe that peasants and aristocrats alike bought into it, no questions asked).

Two centuries later, twenty-two-year-old Tamara co-ruled the Russian land of Georgia, some beautifully wild real estate that fit snugly between the Black Sea and the Caspian Sea. She and her father had a nice tandem thing going; as monarch-in-training, Tamara got a new name, "Mountain of God," and lots of hints from pop, George, about running a country, squelching rebels, and all that.

At twenty-eight, she became sole ruler. In ancient times, this part of the world had worshipped mother goddesses, so Tamara's rule was well-accepted. "A lion's cubs are lions all, male and female alike" is a line from a famous Russian poem thought to refer to Tamara.

Her Majesty, aka "King of Karlti," went through a couple of husbands until at last she found one whose sperm count was high enough to produce heirs. In gratitude, she made him co-ruler—but only *pro tem*.

Like her ancestor Olga, Tammy was an enthusiastic Christian and wanted the best icon that money could buy for Russian Georgia. And what icon would that be? The Holy Cross, of course. She'd just heard that superknight Saladin, the Arab leader who'd mopped the crusaders out of the Holy Land, had a chunk of it, so Tammy offered him 200,000 dinars. Saladin said, "Nyet."

A disgruntled Tammy went back to empire-building and ushering in the cultural golden age of Georgia. Her even more disgruntled first ex-husband tried like mad to depose her several times, but could not. The lioness cub ruled for thirty-four years, establishing a Russian dynasty that lasted for two and a half centuries.

Aethelfled

otherhood was okay, she thought; it was labor that was the pits. After the birth of her first daughter, therefore, Aethelfled politely told her hubby Ethelred "not tonight, not ever, honey" and swore herself to chastity. Unlike other royal couples we could mention, this royal twosome of ninth-century Anglo-Saxon England still worked together. Aethelfled for one couldn't get enough of the battlefield; swords in hand, the two often went into battle. There was no shortage of battles to attend, either: At that time, the island was a real rat's nest of small quarreling kingdoms. Aethelfed's father, known to history as Alfred the Great, had spent most of his life fighting the Danes, who at that time thought of England as "the Viking destination we'd most like to pillage and burn."

After her dad and husband died, Aethelfled kept up the pugnacity. She managed to pull the quarreling Mercians of central England into some semblance of unity and was called "Lady of the Mercians" in gratitude. At forty, this workaholic Saxon spent the next eight years building fortresses, leading troops into Wales, helping her brother Edward out militarily, and negotiating alliances between the equally prickly Brits, Picts, and Scots against the Danish Vikings. For a breather, she captured the strategic cities of Derby and Leicester.

Eventually, Aethelfled came to be looked upon as the unofficial ruler of both Danes and Mercians. Given how well the feminine touch had worked thus far, everyone sort of expected Aethelfled's daughter to be the next ruler.

Sure enough, when Aethelfled finally caught the wrong end of a mace in a battle at Stratfordshire in 918, daughter Aelfwyn inherited the crown. About ten minutes later, however, her uncle Edward conveniently "forgot" about the years of military help his sister had given him, pushed aside female heir Aelfwyn, and made himself king of England.

Ng Mui & Yim Wing Chun

Actress Sally Field may shudder at her long-ago portrayal of *The Flying Nun*, now in the perpetual twilight of worldwide syndication, but the first for-real flying nun was nothing to shudder about—unless you were her opponent, that is. Ng Mui lived during the time of the Ming dynasty of China, famed for vases and other delicate creations. Her times were a lot harder on nuns than on ceramics. Political unrest and bandits meant that religious figures routinely were attacked en route or even in their own monasteries. To keep their numbers from getting seriously decimated, nuns and monks took up martial arts. A feisty figure, Ng originated her own punchy style of Shaolin temple boxing. Her most outstanding pupil? Another nun named Yim Wing Chun, who developed her own system of martial arts, called *wing-chun* after her and still widely taught today. The greatest popularizer of *wing-chun*? None other than that modern figure of kung fu legend, Bruce Lee.

Raziya

Just when female veil-wearing, harem seclusion, and *suttee* (being cremated alive on a pyre with the corpse of your hubby) had really taken hold in India, along came Raziya. Like her ruler father, she loved executive decision-making, and in 1236 she became Sultana of Delhi—at that time, the most powerful state in northern India.

Her dad, Iltutmish, was no slouch on the career ladder himself. Born a slave, he rose to rule Delhi, becoming the greatest Sultan of the Moslem Slave dynasty (at least, that's what his public relations people boasted). In the "who will be the next Sultan" sweepstakes, Raziya stood out early. The fact that her two brothers were feeble-minded party animals helped her chances, of course.

This wasn't an easy time to run India—but then, when has it been a snap? The two main sects of Moslem belief—the orthodox Sunnis and the more radical Shi'ites—were at each others' throats. Raziya tried to stay out of the whole religious mess, but as E. M. Forster wrote centuries later—it's impossible. She ultimately backed the Sunnis but insisted that the law should apply equally to folks of every faith, a policy that made Delhians of every sect absolutely livid.

Meanwhile, however, she turned her attention to more constructive matters, such as digging wells, building roads, issuing her own coinage, and going after trade agreements that would put Delhi in the black for once. A well-educated woman, Raziya could recite the *Koran* (the holy book of Islam) and compose a poem with equal panache. As leader, she built myriad schools and libraries and staunchly supported the creative community.

For four years, Raziya walked the narrow balance beam of power, occasionally resorting to battle when her suggestions weren't peacefully followed. Then her by-now myriad enemies made a move; deposing her, they threw the sultana into prison—possibly in the palace itself.

Always able to think on her feet (even when in leg irons), Raziya went into max-imum persuasion mode. Knowing it would be a tough sell to talk her jailer (who dou-bled as the head of her cavalry) into letting her go, she proposed marriage instead. Dazzled or confused, he agreed. Instead of a honeymoon, however, the two scuttled around, collecting her army for a showdown.

Accounts from historians of the time are, to put it mildly, contradictory. What they all agree on is that Raziya lost her bid to rewin her throne in 1240. Her final hours must have been the stuff of cinematic epic. Riding atop a huge elephant, she led the charge, sending waves of revulsion over the opposing troops at the sight of her totally unveiled face. She was killed in battle by (take your choice) Turkish-backed Hindu troops, the still-mad Shi'ites, or her own queasy army.

With the death of this courageous and commonsensical ruler, the first woman in the world to head a Moslem state, female rule on the Indian subcontinent took a nearly permanent timeout. Not until 1966, when Indira Gandhi stepped up to run India (joined in 1988 by Pakistan's leader Benazar Bhutto) did the key to the ruler's washroom again say "ladies."

Black Farm Woman

Compared to other conflicts, the Peasants' War of the sixteenth century and Black Farm Woman, the "German Joan of Arc," have gotten little attention. It was during the early 1500s, when peasants all over Europe were ignited by the Protestant Reformation and the message of activist Martin Luther; to them, booting out cardinals and priests sounded like hope for a better economic and social future.

By the 1520s, right after Luther got tossed out of the Catholic church and Reformation was on a roll in Germany, humble folks from Bavaria to the Black Forest cut loose, naively proposing an end to serfdom.

At the forefront of the action? A fierce female who styled herself *Schwarze Hofmannin* or Black Farm Woman. She hailed from a village near Heilbronn, a gal with so much vision and enthusiasm for revolutionary struggle that locals thought she had secret powers—or was a witch, perhaps. At any rate, the leaders of the peasant army were only too happy to have Black Farm Woman along to motivate the troops. After centuries of stupefying oppression, Ms. Woman and the other peasants had a genuine hatred for upper-class Germans. Blackie took particular issue with the overdressed high-society women of Heilbronn and was supposedly quoted as saying what fun it would be to slash their clothes off, visualizing them as a flock of plucked geese.

Blackie and the "Bright Band," as her particular gang of 8,000 pitchfork-carrying male and female peasants called itself, soon beat the *lederhosen* off the villagers of Weinsberg and Heilbronn, ousting the establishment, canning the governor, and making the towns official Peasants' War headquarters.

All too soon, however, this people's paradise came to an end. Intent on his own agenda, Martin Luther worked behind the scenes, egging on the princes of Germany to nip the poor-folks rebellion in the bud. As Luther so delicately instructed them: "Whoever can, should smite, strangle, or stab, secretly or publicly."

We don't know what happened to Black Farm Woman after 1525—but we do know that Luther outsmarted himself. The Peasants' War and its outcome made Lutheranism mighty unpopular in those parts; and to this day, southern Germany remains predominantly Catholic.

Brunhilda & Fredegund

ho says women can't hold a grudge as well as men? Not to brag, but sixth-century Queens Brunhilda and Fredegund carried on a forty-year grudge match with enough testosterone to awe even the Serbs and Croats.

Just like the Bosnia-Herzegovina situation today, nobody in Brunhilda and Fredegund's day could agree what to call the region they lived in. Some referred to it as the "Frankish kingdom." Others called it "Merovingian Gaul." The whole thing made everybody edgy. That whole section of Europe hadn't jelled into countries yet but was a still a squabbling, seething crockpot of German, Roman, and Christian cultures.

Upwardly mobile Fredegund had begun life as a palace servant, then at one point, jumped into King Chilperic's bed. Quite a talker, Fredegund: Besides getting her lover to sideline wife number one and kill wife number two, she made it into the winner's circle as wife number three. An active woman, she was only too pleased to handle other troublesome personnel problems for Chilperic. Bribe a bishop? No problem. Assassinate a relative? You got it. Although she had reliable help and her own matched set of asssassins, Fredegund cheerfully took an axe to a couple of those personnel worries herself.

Brunhilda, on the other hand, came from a blueblooded barbarian Spanish family whose relationships were only slightly less tangled than, say, *Days of our Lives*. Brunhilda and Fredegund crossed paths when they got involved with half-brothers; King Chilperic's wife number two, rubbed out to please Fredegund, just *happened* to be Brunhilda's favorite sister.

Did Fredegund give a fig? Frankishly, no. She was on to other things: having baby boys, thinking of various unpronounceable names beginning with "Chlo" for them, overtaxing the long-suffering citizens, and ordering up death *du jour* for a spectacular number of personnel problems.

The two queens collided, verbally and in battle, on numerous occasions. But in 597, Fredegund took the fun out of things by dying of natural causes. A dismayed Brunhilda struggled on, killing as many of her longtime foe's family as she could, but the thrill had vanished. In 613, Chlothar II, one of the few children still left alive in Fredegund's family tree, cornered Queen Brunhilda on the battlefield. He and his army made the queen ride a camel through the jeering troops. As if that weren't humiliation enough at her age, he then ordered her torn from limb to limb—his mommy's child to the last chapter.

Caterina Sforza

She was called "virago," "bastard," and "daughter of iniquity"—and those were the nicer names. Caterina Sforza lived up—or down—to the worst of them. This killer Italian from Forli had a fair face that would stop traffic and a conniving mind that would stop at nothing.

She didn't mind a bit of mayhem, either. Before she even met her first husband, this bride by proxy found herself on the battlefield in 1483, defending his lands in Forli in northeast Italy. She soon expanded her horizons to fighting with the pope, other neighbors, and foreigners like the French.

Caterina often fought on horseback and while pregnant, reluctantly getting down long enough to have eight children by various lovers and husbands. Not that she paid either progeny or lovers much mind: One time when her kids were taken hostage, this spitfire said, "Keep 'em—I can always make more!" She was pregnant at the time.

Among her more peaceful pursuits, Caterina loved making lotions, potions, and the occasional undetectable toxin in her lab. Besides poisons, this early Esteé Lauder compounded her own perfumes and even wrote a book on them.

She was also a shrewd and tolerant ruler in an era of anti-Semitism. After shouting down officials, she used her influence to bring Jewish bankers to Forli, thus giving local businesses a place to obtain credit.

In 1508, an enterprising gal who styled herself "Anna the Hebrew" played Avon lady to this moisturizer-loving royal. Enclosed with a personal letter to Caterina, Anna sent samples of her new black aloe salve, a skin softener. With people of that era being ever so touchy about poisons, Anna hastened to add: "The salve is supposed to be bitter—if a bit gets in your mouth, not to worry..."

If this high-strung celebrity bought her product line, Anna reasoned, her success would be phenomenal—and the association might buy even more protection for the local Jewish community. After all, Bianca Capello, the cosmetic-loving virago just up the road, had kept Jews from getting booted out of Florence.

Good plan, bad timing: Anna's letter arrived just after Caterina had lost a knock-down, drag-out battle with Pope Alex VI over her lands. Losing was bad enough. But then Caterina spent a year in prison being brutalized by the soldiers of the papal army.

Even Anna's very best creams couldn't help the broken woman Caterina had become. The once-vigorous champion of Forli limped off to a nunnery, leaving her lands in the hands of Pope Alex and his greedy son, Cesare Borgia.

Long after the pope's vicious win was forgotten, Caterina Sforza lived on in a fascinating tradition. In honor of her exploits as an Amazon warrior, the dominant figure in the game of chess ever since Caterina's day has been the queen.

"Could I write all, the world would turn to stone."

—letter from Caterina
Sforza to her professor,
written from a prison
cell in Rome

Gráinne Mhaol

he poetic Celtic language is full of words like *twyllforwyn* ("false virgin") so locals in sixteenth-century Ireland had no problem wrapping their gifted lips around names like Gráinne Ni Maille, nicknamed *Mhaol* ("cropped hair") for her Sinead O'Connor look.

Not so the English, who called her Grace O'Malley—and other, less refined names. A few medieval gals with a taste for adventure had made a modest career out of crime on the high seas, but Grace carried it beyond personal gain. For fifty years, this lass of Connacht led the Irish fight for independence from England on the seas. Haul a keel, shiver a timber, shake a cutlass—you name it, she could do it or get it done.

From the Mayo clan, Gráinne married an O Flaithbheartaigh (that's O'Flaherty to you), had three children, and then began her on-ship training aboard a vessel. She rocketed up the main-mast of command; before long, she commanded three raiding ships, which carried 200 fighting men along the Irish coast.

In 1558, Gráinne ran into stormy seas when her bold English counterpart, Elizabeth Tudor, took the throne. The English began seriously messing about in local Irish politics, kicking out Gráinne's husband and killing him. Gracie regrouped to her castle on Clew Bay, more motivated than ever to knock off bloody Brit ships. Eight years later, she took a romantic breather and made a trail marriage with Iron Richard Bourke, another Irish chieftain, pausing oh-so-briefly to have a son Tibbot, who may have been born on board ship.

Gracie just couldn't get enough of fighting—and whipping—the English. After a few reverses, she did a two-year stint in jail, but jumped back in active battle in 1579.

The English tried everything to make Grace say "uncle"; finally they took her son Tibbot and her brother hostage.

Queen Liz herself was sick of battling the irrepressible Irish and their quest for autonomy, so in 1588 she sent Gráinne a conditional pardon. A lot of good that paper did; within months, the Brits were at Gráinne's castle door in full battle gear. Five years later, a fed-up Grace decided to make an end run around the viciously anti-Irish politicos and went to see the English queen, hoping to work out a deal. At their summit meeting, these two powerful women took each other's measure, communicating in Latin and a bit of Welch Queen Liz had learned from her lifetime sidekick, Blanche Perry. Even with her cropped hair, Grace towered over the bouffant and bewigged Elizabeth.

At one point, Grace needed to blow her nose; given a handkerchief, she used it and tossed it in the fire. When Liz told her the cloth was to be put in her pocket and washed for reuse, Grace sniffed that in Ireland they had higher standards of cleanliness. Despite the putdown of her hygiene, Queen Liz was impressed with Gráinne Mhaol. She again ordered her locals in command to stop harassing the Irish leader and her family, to release her son and brother from captivity, and to award Grace a stipend for her old age.

Predictably, those in charge used distance to ignore most of their queen's commands, revving the situation to a red alert. Grace remained in the thick of it, while both sides went at it big-time. After the final defeat of the Irish in the bloody battle at Kinsale, this symbol of the Irish passion for freedom had two years to choke on that bitter pill before dying (like Queen Elizabeth) in 1603.

Amalsuntha

She may have been a barbarian by birth, but Amalsuntha, the daughter of the first Ostrogothic king of Rome, was no ignoramous. A linguist and literature lover conversant in Latin, Greek, and Gothic, she found herself running the Roman empire when dad suddenly crapped out from dysentery.

Besides her capable actions as regent of Italy and the rich islands of Sicily, Sardinia, and Corsica for her ten-year-old son Atalaric, Queen Amalsuntha had a higher goal—the peaceful transition of her barbarian nation into suave, civilized citizens. To show the Goths (who were still belching at the table and picking their teeth with knives) the value of education, she resurrected the crumbling school system established by the Romans. What better way to show 'em "the more you know" than by making her son the nation's model student, she reasoned. Atalaric's bookwormish ways, however, upset the noble higher-ups in the government. They nixed the intellectual curriculum and ordered the kid to get lessons in riding, fencing, fighting, and teeth-picking with a knife. At age eighteen, a confused Atalaric himself died, a victim of tuberculosis, alcohol abuse, and poor self-image.

Mom gallantly continued her solo reign, meanwhile looking around for a suitable alliance by marriage to shut up the good ole Gothic anti-dame game. Her cousin Theodahad looked like a good bet; besides being the only male heir left, he owned more land than anyone else. Best of all, he agreed to her prenuptial demands that he'd be "king in name only." Soon, though, the newlywed relationship went downhill, after Amalsuntha forced her bridegroom to give back some of his ill-gotten property.

Before long, Theo was playing "trade you Tuscany for some gold and a senatorship" behind Amalsuntha's back with Justinian, the emperor of the eastern half of the Roman Empire. By 535, Theo had oozed his way into the Italian kingship. As his first act, he had Amalsuntha whisked from her capital city of Ravenna to a small island, where she was strangled in her bathtub on April 30.

But this farsighted female may have had the last laugh, historically speaking. Theo got less than twenty-four months to savor his "triumph" before Emperor Justinian invaded Italy—why else?—to avenge popular Amalsuntha's death.

Masaki Hojo

For women like Masaki Hojo, being born into the samurai class of twelfth-century Japan was no slice of sushi. Besides learning to wield a mean *naginata*, a long pole with a curved blade at the business end, everyone in this elite caste was very touchy about honor. The least little thing, and you had someone swearing to kill you—"honorable revenge seeking," they called it. Aggression and gore, however, were fine with Masaki, the wife and the most reliable general of the first shogun to rule Japan. (Masaki wasn't the only one heading for the women's showers after a day on the battlefield—two other generals had mistresses who doubled as diehards.) When her shogun died, Masaki took charge, appointing their baby boy as the ruler. Then it was off to the barber for a skinhead haircut, after which *de facto* ruler Hojo became a nun and continued generaling as Ama-Shogun or the nun-general. For generations, she and her descendants continue to rule Japan as the famed Hojo dynasty—serving up stateswomanship and military might rather than roadside sushi.

Urraca of Aragon

"Domestic disputes" took on a whole new meaning when it came to Queen Urraca of Spain and her quarrelsome clan. These folks ate and drank family arguments. Instead of neighborhood shoot-outs, they preferred group activity: war between their armies, mainly.

Urraca was born around 1801. Mom Constance and dad Alfonso didn't waste much time cooing over their baby girl—she was mere backup to their trio of baby boys, who, it was presumed, would inherit the kingdoms of León and later, Castilla. And they would do the fighting. In a pig's eye, as Urraca would say.

Although married young to a French knight who'd come to help fight in the Spanish war of reconquest against the Moors, Urraca wisely kept her armor polished even while birthing two sons. The years 1108-09 were especially busy, wake-wise—Urraca first lost her husband, then her brother Sancho and her dad in battle.

Now queen of León and Castilla, Urraca was revelling in rulership and having the bathroom all to herself, when someone reminded her of that pesky promise she'd made her father before his death. *He* insisted she had to marry the unpopular guy next door, a highly un*simpático* fellow named Alfonso the Battler, who ran the neighboring kingdom of Aragon. Dad's motives were understandable: He thought a guy everyone called "Battler" would do a good job of mopping up the rest of the Moorish infidels.

Marry they did, but instead of mopping, Alfonso and Urraca squared off at each other. To add to the military confusion, Urraca's younger sister Terry decided she wanted to add to the Portuguese real estate she'd gotten at marriage, so she joined the fray. Then a local bishop, trying to be helpful, set one of Urraca's sons on the throne of Galicia, whereupon the kid thought he'd try his hand at armed conflict, too.

The fur was flying so thick in Spain that even the gore-happy crusaders on the First Crusade were repulsed. Traipsing through, many found it tough to get out of the country alive.

For thirteen of her seventeen years on the throne, Urraca battled her obnoxious husband. Besides getting really good at riding and fighting, Urraca issued her own coinage with her mug shot on them—which must have ticked off the Battler something fierce when buying provisions. She solved one problem by simply declaring her marriage annulled, announcing to the Battler: "Bedroom closed, go home!" Mystified, he scuttled off to Aragon.

Only a sexist when it came to her husband, the queen counted on two male advisers—the archbishop of Toledo and her lover, the Count of Lara. (A recent historical study shows that far from being a military figurehead, Urraca made the key policy decisions herself.)

In her late forties, feeling that her rootin'-tootin'-shootin' days were numbered, Urraca threw a ceremony to remind Spaniards who ran the show. At the wingding, she introduced her son Alfonso as successor—and for the *pièce de résistance* had herself recrowned as queen.

Nur Jahan

A pert Persian who started life as Merunissa, she married at age forty for the second time to Emperor Jahangir of India, who'd been googoo-eyed about her for ages.

For a lovesick emperor, his first gift was kind of chintzy. He gave her the new moniker Nur Mahal, meaning "the light of the palace." In a monsoon or two, though, the new Empress Light had the emperor housebroken and eating out of her hand—a process greatly accelerated by his addictions to wine and opium. Pretty soon he'd dreamed up a more grandiose name—Nur Jahan or "light of the world." Empress Global Illumination was really rolling now, and she was to call the political shots of any consequence in India for the next sixteen years.

After she'd employed all her Persian relatives, Nur took to playing polo, minting coins in her name, shooting a few tigers, dabbling in poetry, and putting together a glittering court of beautiful people. In his occasional lucid moments, her hubby worked with Nur to refurbish and add to the unparalleled Gardens of Shalimar in Kashmir. The rulers of India during the Persian Mughul dynasty were especially mad for roses; Nur's own mother was reputed to have invented attar of roses. An empress interested in keeping India green, Nur commissioned countless structures and gardens to beautify the land; she may have even invented the cashmere shawl in her spare moments.

Her main interest, however, was political control; besides running her own cloth and indigo businesses, Empress Light ran the empire. It was a trifle inconvenient, of course, because she had to do so from *Purdah* Command Central inside the harem. (Purdah, or seclusion of women from the general view, was a tenet of Hinduism.

Although Moslem herself, Nur tried to keep the Hindu majority happy by honoring their religious beliefs.)

To keep out of the Hindu public eye, she even hunted tigers from a closed howdah on an elephant's back, sticking her gun through the curtains. (In that humidity, we're talking stuffy—Nur may have felt like having a wine cooler or two herself.)

Emperor Jahangir finally expired of asthma and addictions, leaving the field to Nur and her mess of relatives, in-laws, outlaws, and quarrelsome successors—one of whom included her more-than-fair niece Mumtaz Mahal. The favorite wife (and breeder) of the next emperor, Mumtaz died giving birth to child number fourteen in 1632. And her oh-so-sad husband spent the next twenty-two years building a dazzling white tomb for Mumtaz, which we know as that modern wonder of the world, the Taj Mahal.

Damia al-Kahina

Y ou'd think, after you'd rallied the Berber tribespeople, and taken the Jews who'd gotten tossed out of Spain by the Visigoths under your wing, and beaten a famous Arab general, and led your own army of Jews and Christians and leftover Byzantines to victory over invading Moslem forces, that somebody could get your name right. But no. Variously called Damia, Dhabba, or Dahiya el-Kahina (Kahiya, El-Cahena, and so on), this multinamed woman was a soulful, gutsy leader of the Jerna tribe, headquartered in the beautiful Atlas Mountains around Tunis, North Africa. Most accounts call her gorgeous and wise—the standard eulogistic patter handed down about vixens of the desert. Damia won five years of peace for her people—the only time, incidentally, that anyone would unite North Africa until modern times. Unfortunately, the general she'd sent packing came back for more in 694; at this invasion, Damia gambled on a scorched-earth policy, destroying towns to save them, as the saying goes. Her tactics backfired. Impoverished locals *sans* roofs and camels lost enthusiasm for the cause of independence, and Damia died fighting near a well that is still called "Bir al-Kahina."

Credit Problems
of the Frankly Feudal

Beatriz de Haraña & Felipa Perestrello

Perhaps the most written-about man in history, Christopher Columbus' personal life remains *terra incognita*. What we know about the loves of his life is substantially less than Columbus knew about the location of India—and the scraps we do have about Felipa and the two Beatrices show a side to the admiral that wouldn't win any sensitive male awards.

A lanky vagabond from a humble Italian family who'd made his way to Portugal, Chris got in the habit of going to mass at a certain convent in order to meet Felipa, the daughter of one of Lisbon's tonier families. The two clicked and married; after the wedding, they moved to the islands of Madeira and Porto Santo, where son Diego was born about 1480. Felipa barely lived to thirty. After her death, Chris moved to Spain, then dumped his son with the monks at La Rábida monastery while he lobbied Queen Isabel and King Fernando. Busy with Moor-expelling, the royals gave Chris a "we'll get back to you," and put him on hold for five years.

During that time, the wanna-be admiral hung out in Córdoba, making friends with Jimmy Haraña—and even tighter friends with Jim's cousin Beatriz, a good-looking orphan of twenty. In August 1488, Bea gave birth to a boy she named Fernando—although "Wham bam *gracias* ma'am" might have been more appropriate (it appears Chris had left the building—possibly the province—by then).

When Queen Isabel finally gave the expedition a go-ahead, Chris cruised by Córdoba to give a quick hello to l'il Ferdie, then went south to La Rábida and ordered the monks to drop his older son Diego at Bea's house (once he was safely at sea, you get the feeling).

In 1493, the triumphant mariner returned from his epic voyage to a major fiesta.

He hit Córdoba, said, "I'm back! Thanks for babysitting—oh, and *adios* forever" to Beatriz, and picked up his five- and thirteen-year-old sons. Supposedly to protect his interests while he was at sea, Chris then got his sons appointed as court pages to Queen Isabel.

In case you're thinking that Columbus was a social climber with the emotional range of a jujube, let us note that Chris had fallen for a second Bea during his first voyage. While taking on supplies in the Canary Islands, he met a luscious widow from Gomera whose social connections and physical attributes were equally impeccable. This whirlwind romance lasted *four whole days*. A year later, the love-crazed explorer stopped by Gomera, where Miss Peraza y Bobadilla welcomed his fleet with fireworks, cannons, and most likely, a wed-and-stay-put ultimatum. Not being *that* crazed, Chris took a pass; Bea, however, took some heat when a local guy gossiped that she and C. C. had split a hammock. Bea coolly invited the gossiper to tea; for dessert, she had her servants string him from her rafters, later adorning his own house with the corpse. Her reputation for virtue (and ferocity) restored, she went on to marry a home-based noble.

His Canary Island sweetheart notwithstanding, archival documents show that Chris had a wee twinge of conscience about Bea the first. In 1493, the palimony-allergic admiral gave her the rent concession for the butcher shops in Córdoba—a perk that brought in 10,000 *maravedis* a year. (Sound like meaty money? It wasn't.) In 1502, Chris ordered son Diego to award Bea a similar pension. Meanwhile, sons and father became wealthy and honored; Bea Haraña got into debt, struggled to live on her pensions, and died alone—without so much as a visit from either her son or the man who had probably been her only significant other.

Malinali

A throwaway teen named Malinali (or One-Grass) was the key to the Spanish conquest of Mexico—and all because she was gutsy enough to go after respect. First sold by her parents (both minor rulers of Mayan burgs in the Tabasco region of southern Mexico), she ended up in 1519 as a slave to some coastal Tabascans who didn't seem all that keen on her, either.

Just then, Spanish heavyweight Hernan Cortés pulled up to the curb with ten ships, armed soldiers, and scariest of all, sixteen horses. Racking their brains for appeasement gifts, local bigwigs decided on gold jewelry, five carved ducks, quilted cloth, and twenty female slaves, including fifteen-year-old Malinali. While handing out his own cheesy gifts of cheap beads, Cortés soon saw that Malinali was twenty-four-carat. She spoke several dialects of Mayan and Nahuatl, the Aztec language—which meant she could talk to a Spaniard who'd learned Mayan as a captive from a prior expedition.

Being nearly Easter, Cortés got busy proselytizing, erecting a huge cross and holding religious services—including mass baptism of the Indian women. Newly dunked Malinali got renamed Dona Mariña, "doña" being honorific of high respect in Spanish. Well, maybe not *high* respect in actual deed. Described by an eye-witness as "good looking and intelligent and without embarrassment," Marina got assigned to one of Cortes' captains; a few months later, Cortes himself took Marina for a mistress.

Soon she and Cortés were in hot-and-heavy negotiations with head Atzec, Montezuma. With Marina's vital help, Cortés got rooms full of gold (the Spaniards' main motivation for being there), took Montezuma captive, and ultimately grabbed the gorgeous Aztec capital of Tenochtitlán (now the site of Mexico City).

A quick learner, Marina soon mastered Spanish, meaning that every single word of communication—and interpretation—now went through her. This key player gave the whites a play-by-play on puzzling local customs, showed the Spaniards how to outfox the Aztecs, negotiated the support of rival tribes to fight with the whites, and foiled various plots.

She even made peace with dear old mom, who'd sold her down the river. Being called "Doña Marina" was okay, but what she really savored was her ability to demand that locals call her Malintzin—her given name, plus the "tzin" Aztec honorific only held by nobility. (Cortés himself was called "Malinche" or "Malintzine," meaning "Marina's lord and master," in the Aztec tongue.)

Amid all this activity and bloodshed, our self-made blueblood gave birth in 1522 to Martin, a baby boy. In gratitude for services rendered, new daddy Hernan gave Malinali enough land, gold, and slaves of her own to set her up for life—and then did a little fobbing of his own by getting her to marry one of his *conquistadores*.

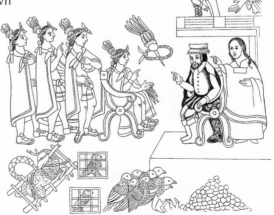

However you called her to dinner, Ambitious One-Grass Malinali-Marina continued to act as right-hand woman, interpreter, and ally in converting the Indians to Christianity until 1551— when, it's said, she died from smallpox, measles, or the flu—just another one of those cheesy gifts from the Spaniards.

Zac-Kuk

A mericans may have a First Lady, but the Mayans of Palenque (a city-state in ancient Mexico) had a First Mother. On October 22, 612 A.D., First Mother Zac-Kuk took the throne. She had crossed eyes, full body tattoos, jade-inlaid teeth, and a nose like a 747—in other words, the epitome of local beauty and fashion. Although Mayans rarely encouraged women to raise their heads from grinding the daily corn, much less put on a crown, a few female rulers did emerge from the more uppity aristocracy. (Details about ruling women are few; until recently, archaeologists had thought the shorter, more rounded images were male priests.)

The astronomically precise Mayans had two calendars: a solar year of 365.242 days and a 260-day sacred year—the length of a pregnancy. For three pregnancies, Zac-Kuk ran things from a mural-bright palace at powerful Palenque. Then her son Pacal turned twelve, stopped playing *pot-to-pok*, the local version of hoops, and became king. Not one to let a teen work without supervision, First Mom kept a grip until sonny got the hang of it. Some researchers think she ran Palenque until her death in 640; however, in Pacal's pyramid tomb, one of the real treasures archaeologists found was a carving of Zac-Kuk proudly handing off the crown to Pacal.

Jimena de El Cid

The way Rodrigo "El Cid" Diaz is fawned over as the first national hero of Spain, you wouldn't suspect the guy had such poor work habits. Someone should have clued in Castillian princess Jimena, a cousin of the king's who married this medieval loose cannon. El Cid loved to make raids on allies and enemies alike; even with his connections, this tactic got him canned. Now with a freelance mercenary for a husband, Jimena got castle-guarding duty while Cid fought for the Moslems, against the Moslems, *ad infinitum*. In 1094, he managed to pick off Valencia, city of oranges, and a relieved Jimena thought: At last! She had five citrus-filled years to enjoy him before he died violently, then brand-new widow Cid became chief defender of her own fortress and Valencia itself. After reorganizing the army (you can imagine how Cid had left it), Jimena held off the Moors for three years before shouting an SOS to her kingly cousin, who obligingly came to the rescue—but accidentally burnt down her sweet-smelling city during the retreat.

Barbara Baesinger Fugger

Fugger was a name to be reckoned with, even back in circa-1450 Germany. The daughter of a stuffy Augsburg banking family, Barbara Baesinger married into the Fuggers, who were big-time merchants in textiles and spices. Eleven children later, bright Barbara had to pick up the pieces when her hubby died young.

Good at juggling career and home life, she educated the kids, expanded the business, and made money, all while personally training the elder sons in management. From the first, she'd pegged her younger son, Jacob, for priesthood. After sending him to Rome to study, Barbara had him turn in his collar when it became evident that sons Ulrich and George needed help in running the family business.

Every bit his mother's son, Jacob was terrific at making money. He jump-started international banking and finance, cornered the copper market, made high-interest loans and low-interest investments for popes and kings alike. Fifteenth-century popes did a land-office business in the sale of benefices (revenue that came with a church position) and indulgences, a "pay-as-you-go" way for Catholics to erase sins, venial and mortal. Jake's biggest coup? Buying the election of Holy Roman Emperor for Charles V—for which Jacob raised 554,000 guilders. (Jacob averaged 54 percent return on his investments; who knows how much his "investment" in Charles paid off.)

Barb's son was now known as Jacob the Rich Fugger, and no snickers either. Eventually the trade in religious indulgences got so disgraceful that activists like Martin Luther brought about the Protestant reformation. And the woman who put it all in motion—the Fugger fortune and the business empire that still exists today—was Barbara.

Frau Nufer

Until Frau Nufer's day in Switzerland of the 1500s, Caesarean birth was a procedure done to try to save the baby once the mother was already dead. According to legend, Julius Caesar's mother Aurelia gave birth to him by this method—but she lived. (Did you notice how it's named after him, not her?) Mrs. Nufer made history by having the first "real" Caesarean. When things started going awry during delivery, the doctor and midwife opted for saving the baby. Her loving husband Jacob objected; when the others bailed, he jumped in. Mrs. Nufer was young and strong, which helped. But the real secrets to Jacob's surgical success were good tools and a working knowledge of anatomy, gained from his trade as a hog butcher. (Plus he cared.) Despite the lack of anesthesia and modern antiseptics, Frau Nufer bounced back to have more kids and live into her seventies—with nimble-handed Jacob by her side, one hopes.

Megg Roper

"**S**weete Megg," her doting father called her. Daddy dearest, also known as Sir Thomas More, England's Lord Chancellor in the time of Henry VIII, was a straight arrow when it came to religious morality. He didn't believe in divorce. (Unlike today, when that belief might cost him an arm and a leg, back then it cost him his head.)

What he did believe in was humanist education for women. Because efforts at female schooling in England of the late 1400s to mid-1500s were feeble at best, More saw to it that his three daughters (and his son) got the best tutor money could buy: himself. An Oxford man, a lawyer, and good friends with Erasmus and other great minds, Tom took Megg and his other kids to the highest levels in Greek, Latin, rhetoric, philosophy, and math. By the age of nineteen, his star pupil and oldest daughter was making translations of Erasmus' commentary on the "Lord's Prayer" into English.

Daddy did have his quirky side, come to think of it. In 1516, he wrote his own version of *Brave New World,* called *Utopia*—in it, he advocated mutual once-overs in the buff for couples about to get married. Not long after, he got a chance to see how his theories would pan out in real life. Early one morning, a whippy young lawyer who'd been sniffing around Sweete Megg came over and asked Daddy for her hand in marriage. With no couth at all, More took him straight to the bedroom where the sisters were sleeping and whipped back their covers and nighties. The commotion— to say nothing of the breeze—woke Megg and her sister up, and they rolled onto their bellies.

The delighted recipient of the double sneak preview gasped, "I have seen both sides!"—then gave Megg a tap on the tush with the romantic words, "Thou art mine."

It's not documented whether Sweete Megg in turn got to study the lawyer's physical equipment—but I'm trusting her father stuck to his utopian beliefs on this. Despite (or because of) this unusual start, the marriage of Megg and William Roper was a huge success. The two were great companions both intellectually and sexually, and Megg went on to educate her own daughters and even the daughter of her nurse.

Besides her other good qualities, Sweete Megg had enormous courage. When her dad was thrown into the Tower of London for his opposition to King Henry VIII, she wrote to him constantly, lobbied for his release, and even fought with the dangerously unstable monarch to the point where she was briefly incarcerated as well. To no avail: Thomas More was beheaded in 1535, when Megg was thirty years old.

Vittoria Colonna

ame artists in Renaissance Italy got gushed over plenty. On occasion, however, the tables were turned. Michelangelo, for instance, couldn't say enough good things—verbally and artistically—about his best friend Vittoria Colonna, the Marchioness of Pescara. (Unlike the "just good friends" disclaimer of modern times, these two really had a platonic relationship. He was sixty-four, and she was forty-nine—which helped.)

A Roman noblewoman of taste and discernment, Vitti's life revolved around poetry, the arts, and religious questions. Married at nineteen, soon separated from her husband by war, they wrote reams of letters to each other. The letters survived, he didn't—prompting the marchioness to mope a spell at an island retreat, writing religious verse. Eventually Colonna embraced life again, becoming a major player in Rome's intellectual life, an authority on Plato, and a published poet at age forty-eight.

What she didn't embrace was another husband. Vittoria became a secular nun (the habit-optional way to go), living in the convent of San Silvestro. From about 1536 on, she and Michelangelo—whose studio was close by—became tighter than ticks. Vittoria inspired Mike to write dozens of sonnets and other poems (which, upon sampling, inspire most readers to be thankful that he wisely concentrated on painting and sculpture!)

More than a poetic muse, however, Vittoria was a spiritual rock, his teacher, his intellectual sparring partner, and the sole person in whom he confided his perplexity and anguish about the rapidly changing world they both lived in, and how to survive in it. Vittoria's simple and fervent beliefs influenced Michelangelo far more than the emotional fireworks of the Counter-Reformation, the Catholic church's attempt at cleaning its own house. In gratitude, he painted three great works for her—today, however, only copies remain of the *Pietá*, the *Crucifixion*, and *Christ with the Woman of Samaria*.

The sole thing Michelangelo regretted about his relationship with Vittoria Colonna was their good-bye. On February 20, 1547, the one woman whose spirit he had communed with for so long, died. As he later told a friend, he greatly wished he'd kissed her face, instead of merely her hand, in farewell.

With sinking heart, she saw yet another sonnet in Mikey's hand

Khadija

Behind almost every great religion founder, there's a great woman. Mohammed and Islam were no exceptions. An orphan who'd had a tough life as a shepherd, Mohammed in his twenties got a job as escort to a trade caravan headed from Arabia to Syria. The owner of the caravan? A widow in her forties named Khadija—an aristocrat from the key crossroads city of Mecca, whose international business via camelback had made her rich. (Belonging to one of the most powerful and wealthy families in Mecca could have helped a tad.)

Not only did this independent woman of commerce like Mohammed's escort services, she dug the man himself. Long courted by upper-class male eligibles around Mecca, she now took the astonishing action of proposing to Mohammed. (You think the Sadie Hawkins thing is unusual now—it was really unheard-of in the world of 595 A.D.).

After marriage, Khadija kept on running her business, with time-outs for six pregnancies. Mohammed kept on running caravans around the Middle East, with time-outs for solitary meditation on spirituality. After receiving a vision in 610, Mohammed told his wife that he was God's messenger for a new monotheistic religion, called "Islam," meaning "submission to the will of God." Converts were called "Moslems," meaning "those who submit." Khadija immediately signed up to become his first (if not most submissive) disciple.

For the next twenty-four years, Khadija supported Mohammed both emotionally and financially, as he struggled to win acceptance for and converts to his religion. A three-time widow herself, Khadija was in favor of legal and economic rights for women. During her lifetime, Mohammed lobbied hard for women's rights and won acceptance for his programs, which sound astonishingly enlightened. Among the rights he established by law for women: Females got to choose their own marriage partners; after marriage, the dowry was paid directly to them—not their parents. The new bride had full and exclusive use of the dowry money during her lifetime and as a nest egg should she become a widow or a divorcee. With Khadija's help, he also developed financial incentives for men to remain married. These laudable achievements were sadly short-term. Worse yet, they weren't written down—none of Mohammed's teachings were, during his lifetime.

After Khadija died in 619, a grieving Mohammed went on to marry twelve women in the next dozen years. After the Prophet's death in 632, the principles of Islam assumed their final written form in the *Koran* and the *Hadith,* a collection of Mohammed's sayings. With their restrictions on female movement and the power given to husbands to administer physical justice in the home, Khadija would be hard-pressed to find her hubby's once-humanistic creed that judged women as equals to men.

Caterina da Vinci

aterina had three problems. She was poor; she was pregnant; and she was pretty darned sure that a certain fast-talking legal-beagle from Florence wasn't going to pop the question. She had a child in 1452—and then got in Mr. One-Night-Stand's face, so he agreed to adopt his illegitimate new son and educate him. Despite Caterina's absence from the scene as a mom, the kid turned out pretty well. His teachers said, "Lacks focus, but boy! can he draw." They didn't even know about the voluminous journals and scientific drawings Lennie had made, much of them in a secret cipher so no one could read them. Eventually Leonardo was receiving coveted art commissions from kings, popes, and other despots with extra *lira*—although, frankly, he would just as soon have kept messing around with futuristic ideas for mechanical devices and making weird paint experiments. By the twentieth century, little old Caterina's boy, born in the hick village of Vinci, was recognized as one of the greatest geniuses of all time.

Lisa di Anton

ere she was, Lisa di Anton, a voluptuous *signora* from the slums of Naples who'd made a good marital catch and, as a consequence, had money to burn for shopping and so forth. But life in Milan was a drag. Her husband was always gone on business trips. She needed a hobby. But what? Then along comes this weird old vegetarian painter who asks to do her portrait. Why not? she thought.

Modeling turns out to be boring, even though he paid for live music and jesters to keep her in a good mood. For years, the artist was still messing around, trying to get her mouth right. In 1507, her husband finally asked if she wanted to come on a long trip to Calabria. She's packed in five minutes—Leonardo and his so-called "portrait" would just have to wait. A few years later, gossip had it that the King of France had paid an awesome sum for the painting of her. Uh-huh—for an unfinished portrait, where the varnish was already starting to make her face look seasick. Today millions line up yearly to see the small, definitely greenish portrait of Mrs. di Anton, now the most famous painting of all time—Leonardo da Vinci's *Mona Lisa*.

Bertha Bigfoot & Bertha

Charlemagne's mom was named Bertha, but everybody called her Bigfoot. When Bert put that big foot down, people listened; her clout at the Frankish court of the Christian emperor lasted until she died in 783. Fond son Charlemagne even named one of his eighteen kids after her. A real family man, Charlie kept his daughters close at hand, refusing to let them marry or enter a nunnery. Being from the Frankish cultural tradition, however, dad had a relaxed attitude about sexual activities. Bertha and her sisters were allowed to have love affairs, even

with men of lower social standing. Dad's rules: Keep it under my roof but out of my sight. When she wanted a winter's afternoon delight with her lover the poet Angilbert, Bertha had to avoid tell-tale footprints from his room to hers. So she slogged through the snow to his digs in the main castle, trudged back to her tower bedroom with Angilbert clinging piggyback, and returned him the same way. (Maybe grandma Bertha got her nickname from a similar routine.) Besides a sex life, Bertha got two bouncing boys from her Angilbert—and, I would guess, some prodigious lats and delts.

Bibi Khanym

That terrible old Tartar called Tamerlane may have walked funny (the proverbial war wound from an arrow), but he was far from lame when it came to bloodshed and brides. Outstanding for being more than a pretty face and a political prize, his wife, Bibi Khanym, made a contribution to history that still stands in Samarkand, Tamerlane's fabled capital on the Silk Road, 1,800 miles southeast of Moscow. The mosque of Bibi Khanym (largest in the world at that time) came into being between 1399 and 1401. The pro-Bibi camp claims that she herself built it with the help of a lovesick architect; the proconqueror faction says that Tamerlane erected the monument in her honor. Whatever the true facts, its huge dome of billiard-ball blue and the picturesque remains of its minarets and arches still tower above the central market in Samarkand, enveloped in a net of scaffolding as restoration efforts proceed.

Borte & Ho-elun

Granted, it's no excuse for becoming a mass murderer, but Genghis Khan *did* come from a dysfunctional family. His mom Ho-elun named him *Temuchin* or Iron. When little Iron turned eight, his parents thought it was high time he quit gobbling all the roast mice at the dinner table and get engaged; accordingly, dad took him fiancee-hunting to another tribe. There Iron met Borte, a ten year old with flashing eyes and a lively face. Son and dad took to her right away, and betrothal negotiations began. Iron's dad offered a horse; Borte's dad raised him a sable cloak; and it was a done deal. In accordance with Mongol customs, Iron stayed with his future in-laws. Before he and Borte even got acquainted, Iron's dad was poisoned by enemies. Iron returned to his mother's yurt, only to find that the tribe had deserted them. While Ho-elun foraged for food, Iron and his five siblings worked through their grief by quarreling and killing each other.

When he turned fifteen, Iron remembered: Hey, I'm engaged! The in-laws were so thrilled at his return that they sent a second sable cloak with the newlyweds for Ho-elun. Speaking of saving your skins: Another vengeful tribe soon attacked their camp. Iron, who was now being called Genghis Khan or Perfect Warrior, was short one horse, so he fled with mom and abandoned his new bride—who was naturally taken captive.

A high-minded Mongol, Borte managed to ignore this gross oversight. Eventually she and Genghis, who was conquering every tribe in sight, reunited. By then, as a break from empire-building, he collected secondary wives as a hobby. Even when the bridal roll call got to 500, however, his respect for Borte and her sound political advice never faltered. And it was among Borte's four sons alone that the blood-drenched legacy of Genghis Khan was divided in 1227.

Kat Ashley & Blanche Perry

In 1537, Katherine Ashley, an English woman with a soupçon of book learning, became governess to a frail royal four-year-old named Elizabeth, who fondly called her "Kat." Her young charge, the daughter of Henry VIII, soon sailed past the tutor—the kid even wrote letters to her brother in Latin. What Kat gave the child was worth more than Latin lessons, however—love and stability. Ashley was there during the bloody comings and goings of King Henry's wives (including the beheading of Elizabeth's mom, Ann Boleyn); his increasingly syphilitic and nutsy reign of terror; the short, sad reigns of Elizabeth's half-siblings, Edward and Mary; imprisonment with her mistress in the Tower of London; and finally, the solo reign of "her" queen. In her scary childhood, Elizabeth had a second rock of Gibraltar: Blanche Perry, who rocked her cradle and later taught her Welch. When she became queen, Elizabeth honored these faithful females. Kat became First Lady of the Bedchamber; Perry was made Keeper of the Royal Books. Both devoted their lives to the luminescent girl in their care who became the greatest careerwoman England ever had.

Mary Sidney Herbert

Repellent as the idea sounded to her friends, Englishwoman Mary Sidney Herbert, the Countess of Pembroke, liked to mess around in the lab. Far from being a dilettante, she was admiringly called "a chemist of note" by Adrian Gilbert, the leading chemist in Elizabethan days.

Chemistry wasn't her only talent. Like many a behind-the-scenes Mrs., the erudite countess took on creative projects for her male kinfolk. When her brother Philip, trumpeted as a poet, a favorite of Good Queen Bess, and "the perfect Renaissance gentleman," died in battle, Mary completed *Arcadia*, his quasi-magnum opus—then she edited and published the thing in 1590.

A patron of poets Ben Jonson and Edmund Spenser, Mary wrote a fairly mean sonnet herself. Indeed, the whole family was quatrain-happy. Mary's son William Herbert was such a heavy backer of Shakespeare that the First Folio edition of Will's plays, and possibly his sonnets, he dedicated to William. (Some also think that the dishy young Herbert may have been Shakespeare's "handsome and noble young man" of sonnets 1–126.)

Besides her ability to juggle motherhood, poetry chores, and stinky chemicals at her palatial digs in Pembroke, Wales, Mary possessed unusual charm and beauty; maybe that's why Jonson's eulogy of her has such a ring of sincerity.

Underneath this sable hearse/Lies the subject of all verse—
Sidney's sister, Pembroke's mother/Death, ere thou hast slain another,
Learned and fair and good as she/Time shall throw a dart at thee.

Simonetta Vespucci

Simonetta made quite an impression in her twenty-one years—but that's what we'd expect from a female with a name like an expensive Italian sports car. This blond bombshell came from the Ligurian coast, today's Italian Riviera but a nowhere place in 1455. Upon marrying a merchant from Florence, she became a poetic inspiration, tournament beauty queen, and a model for painters like Sandro Botticelli, who immortalized her as Flora in his masterpiece, *Spring*. It was artist Piero di Cosimo, however, who really captured Simonetta's ravishing Renaissance look. From her fashionably high forehead (women waxed their hairlines to get that innocently naked frontal lobe) to her snake-entwined necklace (its broken circle symbolizes a life cut short by tuberculosis), Simonetta Vespucci represented the Old World at one of its glorious peaks. Thirty years after her death, her cousin Amerigo would give his name to a brand-New World.

Constance

ew in previous centuries were first-time moms at forty; fewer still, a mother to the likes of Frederick II, who at three inherited Sicily and Germany and later, as Holy Roman Emperor, was called *stupor mundi*—wonder of the world. A Norman princess from a jumped-up family of mercenaries, Connie was pretty stupefied herself, after what she'd had to deal with during labor. In 1194, she gave birth to Freddie in an Italian marketplace for an audience of 200, including fifteen bishops who wanted to make darned sure the heir came from her body. Both Connie and her well-hated husband died when Frederick was small. Indeed, the most intriguing event Connie may have put into motion occurred *post mortem*. When foreign rulers began to exploit Connie's Sicilian holdings, a clandestine group of freedom fighters emerged to clobber them. Some hold that this Sicilian brotherhood morphed into the Mafia—which would make Connie the original Godmother of the *Cosa Nostra*.

Plagues & Other Predicaments

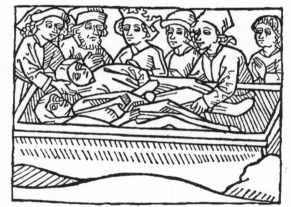

❊ ❊ ❊ ❊ ❊ ❊ ❊

Margarita Fuss

T rue to her surname, Margarita Fuss liked to make a fuss—sartorially, that is. One of Germany's most famous (and noticeable) midwives who practiced in the seventeenth century, she wore oddball duds that included a Hungarian hussar's jacket, a bilious striped skirt, and a gold-headed cane. For cold weather, she would add the *pièce de résistance*—a cape trimmed with bright yellow fur. This early garage sale look, however, was merely eccentricity—or cunning marketing.

Initially, Margarita, or Mother Greta as she came to be called, learned her midwifery skills from her patrician mother, a woman fallen on hard financial times who'd taken to working as a birth attendant to the swells. Fuss followed up her in-house training with studies in Strasbourg and Cologne, apprenticing to several doctors. It wasn't long before Mother Greta became first-string birth coach for the likes of Duchess Sibylla and other fine feathered females. Pretty soon she was on call at a variety of courts throughout Germany, Denmark, and Holland, delivering babies for royal and working-class mothers alike. (Of course, the royals paid better—when they paid; four-star midwives like Margarita frequently charged, but less frequently collected, four-figure fees.)

Midwives in Mother Greta's day, and throughout medieval times, played another seldom-mentioned but highly admirable role. During all-too-common outbreaks of the plague and other epidemics, they assisted doctors. At times, due to high physician mortality, they *became* the doctors. One of the few procedures believed to reduce the pain of plague victims was lancing the swellings in the groin and armpits. This treatment helped draw out the poison and relieve the pressure. Because of medieval modesty, midwives were often called on to perform this procedure for female plague patients. For their extraordinary services, midwives earned special privileges and payments (provided they lived, of course).

The most awesome bout of the plague killed between forty-five and seventy-five million souls in Europe between the years 1346 and 1350. In addition, there were worldwide epidemics of plague in six of the eleven centuries between 500 and 1600 A.D. Margarita saw plague hit four times in various parts of Europe—not, as it happened, in the countries where she worked.

In 1626, church bells throughout Strasbourg rang at the death of seventy-one-year-old Mother Greta. This gesture came from a grateful populace of living mothers and infants who had, thanks to her skills, survived that other great Grim Reaper of medieval times—childbirth.

Mita Lupa

As if fourteenth-century Italy didn't have enough problems for matrons like Mita Lupa, what with crusading husbands who tended to bring home leprosy, and the Black Death, which had killed one out of two Italians. Now southern Italy was getting hit each summer with a plague of spiders. The trouble began in Mita's hometown of Taranto, which gave its name to the fearsome furry little beasties. The only cure for tarantula bites? You had to dance 'til you dropped to the tarantella, a lively dance accompanied by pipes and tambourines. This sweaty activity expelled the venom through the dancers' skin, it was thought. (The phenom-

enon of tarantism may have been due to mass hysteria—or a serious deficiency of village nightlife options.) Live musical healing didn't come cheap, either. Mrs. Lupa was one of many civic-minded women who coughed up to pay the tarantella musicians and other expenses for what came to be called "the women's little carnival." Most women squeezed the money out of their household budgets. Not so Mrs. Lupa. She spent her entire fortune, folks said, to foot the bill for her town's anti-tarantula bash. (Was the word "jitterbug" coined in Taranto, do you suppose?)

Ana de Osorio

Life before quinine was really dire in mosquito-infested South America, so Ana de Osorio, Countess of Chinchon, wasn't all that tickled when her husband came home in 1630 with a new assignment: "Honey, I'm the new viceroy in charge of running Peru—we'll be leaving Spain for lovely Lima."

A few bug-filled months later, a whole lotta shakin' and shiverin' was goin' on. Both the countess and the viceroy came down with malaria and tertian fever. None of Ana's home remedies had any effect. Desperate, the countess decided to try a local cure. Soon she had bands of Peruvians beating the bushes, looking for a certain tree they just knew was around the rainforest somewhere. When they finally located a specimen, the bark with its miracle anti-malarial ingredient, quinine, put Ana and the viceroy on the mend in no time.

In 1638, the diplomats got to return to Spain. Always thinking ahead, Ana threw a little "just in case" quinine bark in her carry-on luggage—and a smooth move, too. Spain happened to be in the midst of a malaria epidemic. Boy did the countess look good, after dosing locals with her personal stash. The magical powder soon got dubbed *Pulvis comitessae*—and the countess' powder and Ana's deeds were raved about in print.

The most lasting tribute, however, came about a century after Ana had brought quinine from the New World to the Old. Swedish botanist Linnaeus developed the Latin-naming scheme for all plants and animals; when he got to the quinine bark-producing tree, he gave the genus name *Chinchona* to nearly 160 species of trees, in honor of Ana, the clever Countess of Chinchon.

Koken & Komyo

Although being a Buddhist nun had kept her in a non-stop whirl of meditation and temple construction, Princess Koken finally agreed to become empress of Japan in 749, when her abdicating dad said, "You gotta help me out here."

For twenty years, she and her mom, Komyo, had been on a real building spree. With dad the emperor's help, they'd established temples and nunneries throughout Japan—and made their capital city of Nara a religious center. Buddhism, it was thought, would also keep natural disasters at bay. Nobody wanted a replay of 644, when a terrible famine led survivors to start a new religion, based on street dancing and drinking lots of sake—and whose supreme being was a giant worm.

More recently, Koken and family had lived through a smallpox plague that had wiped out many nobles in the Japanese court. Obviously, Koken felt, she and mom hadn't done quite enough for Buddhism yet. So the brand-new empress hired 116 priests as demon-busters; completed the world's biggest bronze and goldleaf Buddha statue at the capital; and made the chief priest, Dokyo, an administration czar. Dokyo, a medieval "Dr. Feel-Good," was Koken's own personal physician who'd shot to the top of the esteem chart by curing her in 761 of an unspecified ailment.

To Koken, her actions still didn't seem merit-making enough. So the energetic empress brainstormed further. She came across a religious text, which said that you could be cured of disease and lengthen life if you placed a certain number of written charms in the nearest temple. So Empress Koken ordered up a nice round number: one *million* charms. Japan already had the technology of block printing; even so, her friendly neighborhood printer was stunned by the order. Each charm had twenty-five lines of holy words, encased in a wooden pagoda five inches high. Naturally the empress wanted it yesterday; even with people on triple overtime, however, she didn't get her plague-evading print run until 770.

Temples throughout Japan were promptly awash in pagoda charms, and Empress Koken was just getting compliments on her idea when another smallpox epidemic struck. And wouldn't you know it, Buddha (or perhaps that scary giant worm) had the last laugh: The hard-working fifty-two-year-old Koken was one of its victims.

Some of her charms, however, are still hanging around—the earliest examples ever found of copper block printing. Several temples built by this devout mom-and-daughter tag team also exist in Nara, Japan. And that monster statue of Buddha? At seventy-two feet, Koken's creation still reigns as the biggest bronze in the world.

Jacobina Felicie

A single physician from a ritzy family in Florence, Jacobina Felicie ended up in Paris. The social climate perhaps? Don't think so—Paris of the 1300s was definitely down on dames as doctors. University-trained docs wanted to keep a lock on the profession and its rewards; beginning in 1220, French law allowed only members of the faculty of medicine to practice and needless to say, refused to admit women.

Although Jackie had studied with a master doctor, she got charged with practicing *sans* degree. The penalty was a fine—and excommunication (a "deterrent" that deterred less and less, as more non-university trained healers, male and female, came on the scene). This scenario was repeated several times until 1322, when she went to court to appeal her original condemnation. Gritting her teeth, Dr. Felicie brought eight witnesses—all of whom said that Jackie had refused to take any payment unless or until they got well. That gambit must have horrified the medical establishment.

Felicie also argued that Paris law went against the public good: Women doctors were especially necessary for female patients whose ailments (or modesty—or both) were such that they would not go to a male and would therefore, in all probability, die.

You will not be flabbergasted to learn that neither testimonials nor eloquence carried the day. Jackie, two well-known female surgeons, and several male physicians (all non-U) were again excommunicated and fined. Legally, Dr. Felicie may have gone down to defeat, but it's doubtful she quit. Unlicensed medicine, practiced by determined and dedicated women and men, continued in Paris and elsewhere.

Louyse Bourgeois

You think *you've* got on-the-job stress—in 1601, right after graduating from the super-prestigious French Hotel-Dieu school for midwives, Louyse Bourgeois had the assignment of delivering Queen Marie de' Medici's first kid. It goes without saying, queens and first-time moms are spectacularly tricky customers. What Louyse really sweated, however, was the audience: She had to deliver the goods in front of hundreds of spectators—most of them men. Mom, baby, and audience pulled through fine, though, and Louyse went on to bring over 2,000 kids into the world. In her forties, Bourgeois wrote the first of several books on childbirth—hailed as the most useful obstetrics materials since the time of Dr. Trotula, who had lived 500 years earlier in Italy. Like the previous tomes, Louyse's birth books had a long shelf life, got translated into various languages, and were predictably plagiarized for centuries.

Maria Cunitz

Instead of dinner tables, Maria Cunitz slaved over mathematical tables; in her war-torn part of the world, being a scholar and scientist couldn't have been easy. Growing up in (now Polish) Silesia, this precocious German doctor's daughter lapped up studies in seven foreign languages, math, and medicine, along with dabbling in astrology.

On top of that, she had the fortune to marry another doctor, Elias von Loven, who likewise nurtured and mentored her intellectual talents. Elias also hailed from the same chewed-over chunk of northern Europe called Silesia. After marriage, Maria continued her studies, adding history, poetry, music, and painting to her curriculum.

She had just hunkered down with a nice juicy rainy-day project, namely to simplify the tables of planetary motion published by famed astronomer Johannes Kepler a few years earlier, when a major annoyance hit the neighborhood. The Thirty Years War, which had been spilling equal amounts of Protestant and Catholic blood all over Europe since Maria was eight years old, came to her neck of the woods. There being no ivory towers or bomb shelters handy, she and hubby Elias had to hide out in a religious cloister for some time.

When the all-clear finally sounded in 1648, Maria got back to work and published her results two years later. Her title, which began with the provocative phrase, *Urania propitia sive tabulae astonomicae mire faciles,* ran to twenty-three words. (If this is an example of "simplification," I'd hate to grapple with the original work.)

Frau Cunitz' reputation as an intellectual grew; there was, however, a good news/bad news flavor about her results. It seems she found and corrected many flaws in Kepler's work, but in the complex process she introduced more than a few errors of her very own. Maria lived another fourteen years, carrying on passionate correspondence and long-distance scientific skirmishes with her colleagues over just what motion the planets did have. At least their battles didn't involve real bloodshed—unlike Maria's much-mangled hometown of Schweidnitz, Silesia, and the rest of Europe.

Marie Colinet

A traveling doctor and midwife, Marie Colinet of Berne worked a huge circuit, treating patients throughout Germany. To get medical gigs in 1580, you had to be a "tackle anything" sawbones—a challenge that applied doubly to women. In the course of her rounds, probably moving from place to place in a horse-drawn wagon, Marie did everything from minor surgery to C-sections. The professional highlight of her career came when she encountered a patient whose sight was being threatened by a nasty sliver of metal. Using a magnet, Dr. Colinet deftly removed the metal from her patient's eye—the first time such a technique was utilized. Luckily, a witness was on hand during the operation—her husband and fellow surgeon, Fabricius von Hilden, who wrote up a glowing account of Marie's sleight of hand. You'd think his eyewitness documentation would nail this "female first" down. But you'd be wrong. Before many years had passed, Marie's successful innovation was routinely being credited to Dr. Fabricius—even though his part in the proceedings was his play-by-play description of watching his wife do it!

Theodora

In the bustle and hype of sixth-century Constantinople, you had to be really outrageous to get noticed. Freakishness was a breeze for Theodora, a gutter-snipe-trained actress whose beauty and talent for display gave her the idea for an act that combined porn, dried corn, carefully trained geese, and her next-to-naked body in a hide-and-go-seek performance Byzantines gasped over. A great dancer, an even greater physical comic, this petite forerunner of Evita Peron soon got the hottest parts going in the box-office event of her day—the pantomime theater, which combined the erotic, the vulgar, and the horrifying almost as cleverly as Theodora did.

Theo caught show-biz fever in the cradle. Her father, a bear-trainer at the hippodrome, did a disappearing act when she was a tot. Her mom, burdened with three daughters, encouraged them to dance, show a little thigh, and bring home the bacon. Before puberty officially arrived at Theo's door, she was being paid to do some very grownup sinning as a child prostitute.

After a stint as someone's mistress and a trip to Alexandria, she returned to Constantinople a neophyte Christian—which was fortunate, because soon thereafter she met Christian emperor-in-waiting Justinian. Besides religion, they shared an interest in Theo's physical equipment and charm. But the young bump-and-grind had something under wraps even more shocking than her inventive pornwork—a top-notch intelligence. Around 525, she and Justinian got married to shock, horror, and ill-concealed envy all around. It took an act of Congress to legalize their acts of congress, actresses being marital no-nos for bigwigs.

Like other women with checkered pasts, Theodora put it behind her once married. The new empress immediately got a makeover: a gold-coined crown for height, a long white dress with purple cloak, and a heavily jeweled bib and tucker. The power dressing was just for image, however. She also brought sensible advice, political acumen, and courage to her position.

During the Blue and Green riots fomented by crazed chariot-racing fans turned political rebels, for instance, Justinian panicked and wanted to flee when his troops couldn't control the situation. Theodora said: "You want to *what?* We're all gonna die anyway—might as well do it wearing the purple." Her scathing remarks—and her tactical help in quelling the riots—got Justinian back into command mode. Remotivated troops then made shish-kebab out of 30,000 rioters, who had by this point burned down most of Constantinople.

One good thing about smoking ruins—there are plenty of opportunities to put up some really decent new buildings. With Theo's help, they set to work; some of their efforts—such as the basilica of Santa Sophia and fragments of its stunning mosaics—are still around.

In 542, the dynamic duo's reign was tested by an even bigger disaster: plague. Killing as many as 10,000 people a day, it decimated the city. It tapped Justinian on the shoulder but he didn't dare die—stalwart nurse Theo would be so cross. They both survived the epidemic, only to have Theodora contract cancer at age forty. At her death, she left behind a grieving husband and nation—a final act which would be eerily echoed by the life of actress-cum-"Empress" Evita Peron, 1,400 years later.

Mary Queen of Scots

Two things Mary Queen of Scots adored—endless plots, with herself as protagonist, and the game of golf. Right after her dear second hubby, Darnley, died, she played eighteen holes. Scots applauded her stiff upper lip but wondered a wee bit, given that he was strangled. Darnley's death was just another episode in the drama of Mary's life; next came a fake kidnapping by the probable killer. Mary's acting was superb. She said, "Oh! You beast!" and promptly married

him. Duffer or not, this queen of the greens should have stuck to golf because her rebellions and armies always came unraveled. After a spell in a Scottish prison, she fled to England, where it was back to the slammer. Her cousin Queen Elizabeth wanted to go easy on her, but pesky letters surfaced that seemed to prove Mary guilty of murder, treason, or felonious stupidity at the very least. In 1587, Mary got in the rough again—declared guilty of conspiring against the life of Liz. Her last episode was a Nielsen's ratings winner, though: Mary had a date with the executioner for another sort of hole-in-one.

Courtly Love,
& Not-So-Very

❀ ❀ ❀ ❀ ❀ ❀ ❀

Johanna of Naples

For millenia, women have searched for inner truth, self-awareness, and a fool-proof formula to size up the men in their lives. In 1343, when an optimistic Queen Johanna of Naples married Andrew, a Hungarian royal with a pro-boscis the size of Budapest, she had high hopes that the old alchemical formula "as above, so below" would hold true. Alas, there turned out to be nothing else about Andy that would match the nose in majesty. Deeply peeved, Queen Johanna had her Hungarian strangled—a felonious *faux pas* that got her kicked out of her comfy king-dom in Italy.

The ex-queen then took her entrepreneurial spirit and her interest in things sex-ual to Avignon, France, where she set up Europe's glitziest brothel on some property her family owned. (By a teeny coincidence, Avignon was at that time the headquar-ters for one of the two popes of the Catholic Church.)

Her first goal: to make points with the female entrepreneurs who were already freelancing their sexual wares in Avignon. They wanted their own version of the Teamsters' Union? Bravo, said Johanna, and she signed papers that gave the ladies of the night their own association and membership ensignia—a bit of red braid on the shoulder. That done, it was a piece of croissant to fill her luxury bordello with the highest-quality flesh *artistes*.

To maintain cathouse cachet, Johanna set up house rules, which included Saturday STD exams and in-house quarantine for women found contagious or in the family way. She may have been a party-all-nighter herself, but Johanna ran her busi-ness according to good Catholic guidelines—no birth control, no abortions, and guar-anteed care for any offspring her ladies brought forth.

After managing her Gold Card–only establishment for a year or so, Johanna sold it to a salivating buyer—none other than local Pope Clement VI, who continued to run Johanna's joint under the name "The Abbey."

Century 21 would have paid a mint to have this royal businesswoman in one of their mustard-colored blazers. Besides getting asking price cash for her place, Johanna finessed a pardon from the pope for all past sins—including that impetuous murder of poorly endowed Andy. The only trick she missed? A papal pardon for the numerous fleshly sins fun-loving Johanna went *on* to commit.

Why yes, there is a special rate for bishops

Heloise

Emasculating women? The Dark Ages had 'em. But in Heloise's case, the emasculation was totally unintentional. *Her* hints from Heloise would have read: "If you jump into bed with a clergyman, never get pregnant. And forget about telling your relatives!"

At age seventeen, this bright young Parisian intellectual began studying philosophy with Peter Abelard, twice her age and the hottest celebrity theologist in twelfth-century France. Pete's tutoring quickly turned into something more earthy, unwittingly aided by Heloise's clergyman uncle, who naively rented him a room in their house.

There was a flaming row when Uncle Fulbert found out about the sex—and a worse one when Heloise turned up preggers. After she gave birth to a son named (shades of the 60s!) Astrolabe, Pete promised Unk he'd marry Heloise if it could be kept secret; a calculating sort, Abelard didn't want to jeopardize his sunny career possibilities in the church. So far, only *un peu bizarre.*

At this juncture, however, to paraphrase Cool Hand Luke, a major failure to communicate took place. Abelard took Heloise to the convent where she'd been educated, ostensibly to hide out until their wedding, where the lovebirds did a more than little aardvarking in a quiet corner of the refectory.

It's not clear whether the two actually married or not. What is clear is that fond uncle got the notion that Mr. Hot-Cassock was abandoning or disgracing his niece. (And maybe he was.) At any rate, Uncle Fulbert took action. He hired a couple of dagger-equipped suits, who broke into Pete's room one night and castrated him.

The horrified lovers immediately joined his-and-her religious orders. (Actually,

Abelard leaned on Heloise to join up and waited until she did, before entering a monastery.) Peter did stints at several monasteries, becoming a scholarly monk whose teachings continued to irk the church—and finally got himself denounced as a heretic. For her part, Heloise reluctantly embraced nunhood, eventually becoming abbess of Paraclete convent, founded by Peter in 1129.

Although nothing else could smolder, their correspondence went on hot and heavy for years. Despite its contradictions, the Heloise and Abelard "romance" became one of the most-repeated stories of their age and later centuries.

Judging by the intelligence and fire displayed in her eloquent letters, Heloise deserved better than a self-righteous and randy religious man. Chemistry is chemistry, however, even when you cover it with a habit. Her passion for Pete burned unabated throughout her life, and she was buried by his side, twenty years after his death.

> *"I was more pleased with possessing your heart than with any other happiness...the man was the thing I least valued in you."*
>
> —first letter written by
> Heloise to Abelard

> *"Banish me forever from your heart, it is the best advice I can give you. "*
>
> —letter from Abelard
> to Heloise

> *"I ought to deplore what we did—but I sigh only for what we have lost."*
>
> —letter from Heloise
> to Abelard

Trotula of Salerno

The doctor who dazzled the Dark Ages, Trotula studied and later practiced medicine during the eleventh century at Salerno, Italy's famed medical school—the first of its kind in medieval Europe. Doctoring ran in her family. This bright Neapolitan woman married a sawbones named John Platearius; their sons Matteo and John went on to make it a doctor dynasty. Around the breakfast table, she might have been called "mama mía," but elsewhere, even her sons referred to her as "Dr. Platearii" or "learned mother Trocta." Son Matteo was careful to point out in writing that his mom was a *magistra* or university-trained doctor, not merely an *empiric* or midwife.

Trotula made the study of women her specialty; among her good deeds, she pioneered surgical techniques for repair of the perineum, a critical piece of female anatomy often damaged in childbirth, as any postpartum mother with an aching backside knows. Trotula also wrote two important medical books: *The Diseases of Women,* often referred to as *Trotula Major,* which covered obstetrics, gynecology, and general medicine; the second, *Trotula Minor,* dealt with skin treatments. Over one hundred manuscript copies of her writings still exist—and her work was consulted and plagiarized for centuries.

Much of her advice remains valid. For instance, the good doctor advocated the use of opiates to ease childbirth pain and prescribed hormonal treatments (made from animal testicles) to regulate menstruation and overcome sterility. She also was very big on cleanliness—its lack being a leading cause of mother/infant death until the twentieth century.

Not all of Dr. T's medical palaver was so high-minded, however. Her most popular contributions may be the ones she made to the state of virginity. In medieval times, as now, young virgins sometimes turned into young, hot-to-trot vixens. Once they had trotted, so to speak, the delicate issue of their modified equipment became priority number one when they got engaged. For her maidenhead-obsessed age, the ingenious physician invented a number of remedies for making virgins almost as good as new—if not as good as gold.

Dr. T's most useful prescription called for putting a leech on the area in question, the day before the wedding. Although medieval folks thought nothing of slapping on a leech or two for a quick "bleeding" (their equivalent of two aspirin), the make-a-virgin procedure was trickier. Keeping track of the darned thing (leeches move fast) was key. Virgin wanna-bes also had to make sure they removed the blood-thirsty little critter before they got too many quarts low—as Dr. Trotula would second, a corpselike pallor makes it really tough to be a radiant bride.

Walladah al-Mustakfi

The original "I did it my way" woman, Walladah al-Mustakfi managed to trash the conventional ideas of what a nice Moorish girl in eleventh century Andalusian Spain should and shouldn't do. Odds are good that she got the money to behave as she pleased from her father's side of the family—he was caliph of Córdoba. Rumor has it that her mom was an Ethiopian slave, possibly a Christian—neither demographic noted for its affluence in that time and place. Pop conveniently popped off when Wallie was about thirty, assassinated by his own enraged people over some unpleasantness he had perpetrated.

By this time, Walladah was famous as a poet, writer, singer, and the leader of a brilliant literary circle—the Gertrude Stein or the George Sand of her time. She completely flouted the Islamic notion of wearing a veil as every dutiful Andalusian maiden of the day did. Instead, she designed her own unisex apparel. By the sound of it, she favored a sheik of Araby look, often wearing a lavishly embroidered jacket upon whose sleeves was calligraphed, "I will let my love touch my cheek, and I feel free to give my kisses to whomever asks for them."

Walladah's kisses did in fact get rather wide distribution; among their recipients were lovers male and female. One such passion was Ibn Zaydun, a big noise among Hispano-Arab poets herself, who really fell for Wallie. To lend further enchantment, these two creative souls conducted much of their romance at a distance: Whole camel-loads of their correspondence in verse still survive. Because of the force of her personality and her immense talent, Walladah seems to have called the shots, romantically speaking.

When she herself reached middle age, love's thunderbolt hit again; this time, it was Wallie who went up in flames. Her new amour was young 'n gorgeous Muhjah al-Tayani, who had been mentored by Wallie to reach her poetic potential.

Decade after decade, disgruntled Andalusians kept predicting dire things for the perennially single poet with this AC-DC sort of lifestyle. None materialized. As a final guffaw in the face of convention, Wallie's last years were spent in the plush pad of an admiring businessman, who cosseted her until her death in her serene seventies.

Sei Shonagon & Lady Sarashina

As the year 1000 approached in Europe, women and men of every social class put their lives on hold, awaiting dire millenium events. In Japan of that same era, the fever was more Linda Lovelace than apocalyptic. Readers tore into books by Sei Shonagon and Lady Sarashina, contemporaries who used beautifully literary language to retail the dirty doings of the royal court. In the bull market of trashy memoirs written by former insiders, the most popular tell-alls were penned by women—most using that literary litigation avoidance standby, the pseudonym. Once a lady-in-waiting to the empress, Sei wrote a blazing bedroom work called *The Pillow Book*, its scandalous episodes based on her own risqué research with courtly (and not so courtly) lovers. Lady Sarashina, whose social position at court had been more marginal, took the "wallflower at the orgy" approach, whining beautifully about her inner life, from her dreams to her loneliness in old age. In the intervening thousand years, *The Pillow Book* has lost ground but *Sarashina Nikki* has become one of the classics taught in Japanese schools.

Alessandra Macinghi

The Italian Renaissance saw many singular supermoms, who tackled the challenges of raising a family, engaging in business, fighting political battles, and dealing with the vicissitudes of life—all without a single car pool, child psychologist, or cell phone.

Alessandra Macinghi was one such stellar mama. Born in 1406, this flower of Florence married Matteo Strozzi at sixteen and bore seven kids in eleven years. When the mean Medicis came into power, her husband Matteo, a very big man around city hall, got banished; without turning a hair, Alessandra scooped up her brood and followed her man into exile outside Italy. The year 1436 proved to be a very bad one: Matteo died, as did three of the kids; to add to her woes, Alessandra found herself pregnant. She and the rest of the family returned to Florence, where as a widow with four children she struggled to hold onto what was left of the family fortune and eventually to deal with the exile of her sons. (After banishing men like Matteo who had the "wrong" politics, boss Medici also banished their sons as soon as their tickler files indicated they were twenty-one.)

Besides her other chores, Alessandra had to spend twenty years corresponding with her boys. As her surviving letters show, Mrs. Macinghi made maternal bossiness by mail into an art form. To enable her sons to start businesses or become apprentices, she cut corners, made cunning business deals, and got the very best tax advice (urgently needed in those often nondeductible times).

She didn't overlook the girls, either. Alessandra worked tirelessly to negotiate the most advantageous alliances she could network or nudge. Her sons took more work to marry off. For years, Mom was in there pitching and rounding up candidates, whose figures and dowries both had to be of a pleasing plumpness.

In a letter to her oldest son, Phillip, she finally took a hard line: "I pray to God that he frees you from your fears—if all men were as afraid of marriage as you are, the world would have long since died out!" When Phil did tie the knot, Alessandra got what every Italian supermom craves—grandkids under her roof and a new daughter-in-law under her thumb.

The widow Macinghi was no saint; she didn't have much compassion for humbler folk. As her letters indicate, when poor tenants, bumbling servants, and household slaves couldn't cut it, they were out on their ears. But she was a heck of a matriarch. In another letter to a son, she chuckles: "If I had no other interruptions in my work than my grandson, that would be more than enough, but I get so much pleasure from it. He follows me everywhere, like a chicken following a hen."

Parnell Portjoie

If you were headed for the Bankside district of London around 1290, you could only be looking for one thing: sexual healing and dealing. Bankside brothels were famous—and none more so than the establishment of Parnell Portjoie, whose "door of joy" was open to all. She and her pimp, Nicholas Pluckrose (pure poetry, aren't they, the handles used by sex workers in jolly olde England), ran this busy love nest for an absentee owner. Its profits were a Godsend—or maybe that was just inside pull. As the municipal records still show, the behind-the-scenes boss happened to be a local bishop of the Church of England.

Artemisia Gentileschi

"As long as I live, I will have control over my being." That vow came from the lips of Artemisia Gentileschi, well-known in the seventeenth century as a superb painter—and the plaintiff in a Rome rape trial as sensational in its day as anything in the twentieth century.

The daughter of well-known painter Orazio Gentileschi, Artemisia showed her creative abilities early. After teaching precocious Artie everything he knew, dad looked for a tutor to teach his kid perspective; he settled on Agostino Tassi. Artistically adept, Tassi may have been, but his real talents lay in darker areas. Somehow dear dense old dad overlooked Tassi's criminal record—which included a conviction for having rigged his wife's murder! Lessons between the eighteen year old and the artistic ruffian began, at first chaperoned by another woman—whom Tassi found easy to get rid of long enough to hit on Artemisia. Seduction was a hard sell to this strong-minded teen, and Tassi raped her.

When he found out, dad pressed for marriage. (Oh, for a parent with some sense.) At that point, Tassi laughed in his face—so Orazio pressed charges and the matter came to trial. Despite repeated cross-examination, Artemisia was adamant about her sexual assault and its details. She might have lived during the Renaissance, but trials in her day still had a chilling Dark Age twist. Instead of lie-detector tests, material witnesses got tortured for veracity, right on the witness stand. As 1612 dragged on, Artemisia underwent agony for five months; prosecutors used the thumb-screw on her—a device both portable and excruciatingly painful. (Transcripts of her horrifying trial still exist, by the way.) Innocent plea notwithstanding, Tassi did get convicted—but he won an acquittal after a mere eight months in jail. (Sound terribly *deja vu*?)

After her Marathon trial in Rome, that most gossipy of cities, Artemisia could have curled up in a self-pitying fetal state. Instead, she split for Florence, where she set herself up as an artist, becoming the first woman in the painters' guild, and attempting a short-lived marriage with Pietro Vincenzo. (Their daughter, Palerma, inherited the Gentileschi genes and painted, too.)

Artemisia's art echoed her life and gained strength from it. A Baroque artist of the Caravaggio school, she painted shattering scenes of human drama, with strong highlights and inky blacks. Besides portraits, Artie took hackneyed, done-to-death biblical subjects, like Judith killing Holofernes, and turned them into . . . autobiography. She did six versions of the obviously therapeutic Judith story; through her work, Artemisia gained the most profound revenge of all on her attacker—an artistic legacy that endures to this day.

She even managed to put aside what Papa Orazio had put her through. At his pretty-please, in 1638 she joined the now-sickly painter in London to collaborate with him on a major commission for England's King Charles.

Much of her life, Artemisia lived as an independent woman, handling both the business and artistic aspects of her career. It's clear she knew her own worth. A few years before she died, Artemisia sent a painting to one of her blueblooded patrons, with the simple statement: "This will show your Lordship what a woman can do."

"You will find the spirit of Caesar in the soul of this woman."

—letter to a patron

Bianca Capello

Bianca Capello, whose last name means "hat," threw hers into the ring early. By age fifteen, this teenager found her hometown of Venice and her noble upstanding family a great big snore. After some secret snuggling with a clerk, Bianca discovered a stork in her future. No problem: She blithely eloped with young Pietro to his hometown of Florence, where, she hoped, the real action was.

Because of the Capello family's clout, the Venetians caused quite a stink, demanding the teen's return. "No go," the Florentines said. It wasn't long before this sixteenth-century siren caught the eye of a skinny, short, morose fellow named Francesco—one of the married but wandering de' Medicis. After a quick remodel of a family mansion lying vacant, Francesco installed Bianca in it as his new mistress. (Mr. Sensitivity even put her "Capello" family crest above the front door—where it can still be seen today.)

A fun-filled seven years sped by. Although there wasn't a peep out of Bianca's hubby Pietro, who was kept well-greased with spare change and job favors, the lovers grew a bit tired of the secret liaison. In 1572, Pietro turned up dead, and Bianca and Frankie started turning up everywhere. (Frankie's Austrian wife, homesick, unwell, and thoroughly ignored her whole marriage, wasn't consulted.)

At long last, Bianca's man got the top job—his dad died, and Frankie became Grand Duke of Tuscany in 1574. *Molto bello*, thought Bianca, *but I'd better consolidate my position with, say, a baby boy Medici.* Unluckily for Bianca, she wasn't pregnant just then—but that didn't stop her. She told Frankie she was expecting; through dextrous sleight-of-hand with layered clothing and a lot of cloaks, she was able to pull off the pseudo-pregnancy. After a secluded "birth," Bianca triumphantly revealed a brand-new "son"—freshly taken from a new mom of the working-class. Always good with details, Bianca carefully expurgated her various accomplices in this affair—only to have Frankie learn the truth anyway.

Not being a vindictive sort (unlike the rest of his murdering family), he just cut the kid out of the line of succession. Three years later, Frankie's wife (remember her?) died, allowing Frankie and Bianca to get married. Joy in Florence. Greater joy in Venice, where the Capellos could hold their heads up at last. Smooth sailing ahead for bright-eyed Bianca, barely in her clear-skinned prime at thirty, and now the Duchess of Tuscany.

Elope in a gondola? But I'm gonna need my wardrobe...

Our Venetian hat trick had nine years to gloat. Then, after an especially delicious hunting banquet hosted by Frankie's younger brother Ferdie, Bianca and her husband both died. Suddenly. To absolutely no one's astonishment, Ferdie stepped up to the plate as Grand Duke.

Buran

Who cares about ships—hers was the face that launched a thousand eggplants. Possibly the most beauteous in Baghdad, Buran wedded a ninth-century caliph in a wingding that was called the biggest bash of their times. To imitate an Arab poet's much-admired description of a glass of bubbly, wedding attendants poured thousands of pearls over the groom's head as he sat on

a carpet of woven gold. To honor local passion for purple veggies, the cooks invented and named an eggplant dish after Buran. In no time, Buran was a household word from Syria to Spain. After whomping up the millionth Buran eggplant dish, however, cooks started getting some major grumbling—until one visionary devised a queenly recipe *sans* the veggie. Chefs from Greece to Croatia are still happily cooking dishes with some variant of Buran's name today—some with nary a whisper of aubergine. And now you know why.

Bertrade

Bertrade was in a fifteen-year-old snit—and no wonder. She'd been forced to marry the French count of Anjou, who was fifty if he was a day. The old geezer had been down the aisle five times, too. Finally, however, the newlyweds got a houseguest worth bragging about: King Philip I. Although married, Phil had pinup potential and was younger than twenty-one, so Bertrade could, like, relate. *Vive les hormones:* A nanosecond after Philip left, Bertrade followed him, disguised as a page. Then the couple talked a bishop into a blue-plate special: annulling their prior nuptials and marrying them to each other. That done, the kids settled down to domestic bliss. Slight hitch: While reviewing documents, the pope declared theirs about as good as bogus I.D.s, so he threw Phil out of the church. In 1090, excommunicated royals made very uncool role models, so Bertie and Phil went back to court. And back. And back. You think the judicial process is achingly slow today? Bertie reached the ripe old age of twenty-seven and had three kids before the Parisian court finally OKed her divorce, nullified Phil's first, and declared their twelve-year marriage *c'est si bon.*

Elizabeth, Margaret, & Margery Paston

hanks be to family packrats who saved three generations of Paston family letters and legal documents dating from 1422 to 1509—over a thousand have survived to our day. No trite "Wish you were here" postcards from this upper-middle-class Norfolk clan. This family could even get a rise out of Oprah's most jaded audience; their days and nights were full of paternal calculation, maternal abuse, sibling anger, and filial defiance.

Daughter Margery married "beneath" her, to Richard the family steward, who sounds like quite a decent fellow. In a stealthy note to Margery when the two are already married but haven't sprung the news to the folks, he says: "This life we now lead is neither pleasure to God nor to the world, considering the great bond of matrimony that is betwixt us and also the great love ... wherefore I beseech Almighty God to comfort us as soon as it pleases him, for we that ought of very right to be most together are most asunder..." Once they got word of the wedding, the parents had a hissy fit and refused to see Margery ever again. Stuffy big brother John seemed particularly incensed over the fact that his sis had to stoop to (horrors!) retail, selling candles and mustard. They even had the bishop run his most excellent guilt trips on her—but she held firm. Margery may have gotten her courageous example from her sister Elizabeth.

Several years earlier, both parents physically abused Elizabeth, trying to make her marry a doddering old man with deformities whose chief asset was his pocketbook. For three months, they locked the girl in a dark room without food and beat her several times a week, and in the English of the day, "brok hir hed in two or thre places." Bloody but definitely unbowed, Elizabeth held her ground, left home, and ultimately married twice—both of them happy alliances, which incidentally made her one of the richest women in medieval England.

Albeit a bit of a nightmare from her daughters' point of view, family matriarch Margaret had heavy responsibilities. After her husband, John, got elected to English Parliament in 1460, Margaret had to manage the family farm plus the Paston wool and malt businesses, which she competently did. As head of the estates in his absence, she also ran a judicial court for local village disputes.

Tough love, Paston family style

Country life wasn't all smooth sailing, either. Besides contending with the kids and the businesses, their property got attacked more than once by armed men—some of them neighbors with whom the Pastons had had a falling-out! Unflappable even under siege, Margaret held the fort. During a lull, she'd fire off a note to John with a request to send more crossbows please, and two or three poleaxes pronto. On one occasion, a band attacked the manor and literally pulled it down around her ears. Just another day in the Paston life of medieval England—as her letters attest.

Juana La Loca

In the royal marriage-go-round, she could have been stuck with Charles the Bald or Pepin the Hunchback, but Princess Juana of Spain, the pet daughter of Queen Isabel, lucked out. Her brass ring? Phillip the Fair, monarch of the Netherlands and definitely a Dutch masterpiece. Nine years later, another brass ring: Upon her mom's death in 1504, dark horse Juana became Queen of Spain, all the expected heirs having expired.

All this luck, plus giving birth to six kids in a row, equalled major stress. But the real straw for moody Juana, already being compared to her melancholic grandma, was Fair Phillip's wandering eye. A few ugly scenes later, after Juana had made a very public haircutting and scratching attack on a possible blonde rival, the Dutch treat

started locking Juana into her chambers. Padlocks didn't dampen Juana's crazy love for Phil, however.

When Phil died unexpectedly at twenty-eight, Juana came completely unglued. To get her mind off the tragedy, she toured Spain for three years. The snag was, she dragged Phil's embalmed corpse along with her—and then found she couldn't get him out of her mind *or* her nose.

In due course, Juana's dad Fernando, the king *pro tem*, installed locks at Tordesillas castle, where his poor mad daughter got to share cozy chambers with the by-now exquisitely dead

Phillip. Juana didn't mind—she had Phillip all to herself *and* her music. For the next forty-seven years of her long and locked-up life, her jailers at least had the compassion to surround La Loca with a variety of musicians and singers. (No report on how the boys in the band liked the venue—or if they ever got to leave, either.) Even today, historians don't know if Juana's insanity was genuinely lifelong—or a politically convenient excuse for others to rule in her stead.

Gwerful Mechain

A Welch poet who lived in the latter half of the fifteenth century, Gwerful gave everyone an earful with her frank and eloquent poems on female sexuality. Ms. Mechain may have been a hit in medieval times, but it appears she's a little too pungent for modern sensibilities; her work is noted for its exclusion from most Welch poetry anthologies. (Anthologists seem to have fewer qualms about Welchmen like Dafydd ap Gwilym, whose poetic paeans to his own penis have found a home in many a poetry collection.)

Although she wrote poetry on nature, taverns, and other subjects, Gwerful really hit her stride when she wrote a ditty with the catchy title of Cywydd y cedor, or "The Female Genitals." As anyone who has tried to write poetically about sex knows, it's not that easy to celebrate feminine biology. Gwerful pulled it off, however; check it out for yourself.

Louise Labé

Born into a Lyonnaise ropemaking family and married into another, Louise Labé lassoed whatever she wanted from life. She actually believed women could do or learn anything—a timely concept for France of the 1520s, which had just been mauled (again) by the Black Death.

Paris' only cultural rival, her home city of Lyons was the focal point from which the French Renaissance spread. Her lower middle-class beginnings notwithstanding, this persuasive Frenchwoman managed to get herself a marvelous education. As she once wrote to a friend, "Since a time has come, Mademoiselle, when the severe laws of men no longer prevent women from applying themselves to the sciences and other disciplines, it seems to me that those of us who can, should use this long-craved freedom to study and to let men see how greatly they wronged us when depriving us of its honor and advantages. And if any woman becomes so proficient as to be able to write down her thoughts, let her do so and not despise the honor but rather flaunt it instead of fine clothes, necklaces, and rings. For these may be considered ours only by use, whereas the honor of being educated is ours entirely."

The free-spirited Mrs. Labé didn't confine herself to intellectual capers, either. Married young to local twine czar Enne Perrin, at twenty-two she took up martial arts and became a superlative horsewoman and archer. Louise got a kick out of jousting, once even participating in a Lyons tournament in honor of the king's visit. During the siege at Perpignan, wanting to help her countrymen, she rustled up a flattering suit of armor and fought for them. This was no case of defending her own hearth and home, either—Perpignan lay some 300 miles south of Lyons.

In her pursuit of learning experiences, Louise went after love as headlong as she did everything else. And then she wrote about it. Sometimes shocked at her honesty, certain males interpreted her candor to mean that Labé was turning her hand (and other body parts) to tricks, as a courtesan. I doubt it. Louise attracted her own circle of creative friends; the salon of "the beautiful ropemaker" became one of the most famous in France. Her affairs with an array of poets, and her husband's acceptance of them, were *trés* French. (She did have a notorious fling with a local attorney, but hey—anybody can make *one* mistake.)

Louise wrote her passionate sonnets in Italian and French, distilling her experiences into poetry as fresh and sparkling as a split of fine champagne. Some of her verses sound like contemporary song lyrics:

> *Kiss me again, again, kiss me again!*
> *Give me one of the luscious ones you have,*
> *Give me one of the loving ones I crave:*
> *four hotter than burning coals I shall return.*

Always a realist, lion-hearted Labé knew equally well the downside of love, as this memorable line indicates:

> *a woman's heart always has a burned mark.*

Tullia d'Aragona

By the sixteenth century, when Tullia d'Aragona peddled her glamorous wares around Rome, Ferrara, and Florence, the GNP of the Italian Renaissance owed an astonishing amount to the prostitution industry. In Venice alone, 11,000 hookers serviced a city of 150,000. When one pope tried to rid Rome of strumpets, boosters complained that the place would lose one of its greatest charms.

Now Tullia was no tawdry one-night stand. A culture maven, she lived in one of Florence's high-rent districts, her beautiful villa filled with books and works of art. Known as the hostess with the mostest (action, that is), Tullia kept dinner conversation sparkling, witty, and erudite. As the well-subsidized biological daughter of a cardinal, she had resources, which let her become a poet of sorts and the leader of a popular salon on platonic love.

Tullia wore the cutting edge in fashion—and that, in fact, was the major gripe put forth by well-to-do wives and other respectable females throughout Italy. Since the upscale sellers of sensual delights wore fabulous jewels, sumptuous furs, and clothes identical to their own, nobody could tell who played for pay and who didn't.

The high-ranking women of Florentine society put *molto* pressure on the Grand Duke, who finally decreed that local courtesans had to wear a veil with a yellow stripe on it, which quickly got nicknamed "the whore's mirror."

In this manner, European courtesans came to resemble taxis. In the city of Florence, you flagged down the one with yellow stripes; in Bern, Switzerland, it was the women wearing green coats; in Toulouse, France, white duds indicated a professional.

Tullia, however, had such pull with the duke that he gave her the green light, allowing her to be seen in public without a "whore's mirror."

Being a suavely sophisticated and aristocratic dirty old man, naturally the duke didn't put it in quite such colorful terms: "In recognition of the rare knowledge of poetry and philosophy which is hers to the joy of esteemed minds," he said, "Tullia need not observe the regulation."

Lady Castlehaven

Spousal rape may seem like a twentieth-century issue, but medieval women endured it—and one gutsy soul took her husband to court. In a 1631 case whose outcome shocked England, Lady Castlehaven charged Lord Audley with rape. As the trial revealed, Audley not only liked forced sex, he liked to watch it; Lady Castlehaven had also been assaulted by Skipwith the stableman and Broadway the butler, while her husband helped hold her down. After the Broadway episode, she tried to kill herself, but the butler got the knife and broke it. As rebuttal, the accused rapist issued dire warnings regarding what would happen to dear old England if mere wives and servants were allowed to testify against male heads of household. Despite this bold defense, Lord Audley was convicted on both charges and divested of his head in short order—a deterrent if I've ever heard one.

Rosa Vanozza

osa Vanozza and other *signorinas* on the make knew that the pleasure-seeking tone of fifteenth-century Italy was often set by the most powerful pleasure seeker: the pope *du jour*. With that in mind, Rosa set out to be the CEO (Chief Erotic Officer) of a Catalan priest named Rodrigo Borgia (yes, *that* Borgia), who bought himself the papacy as Alexander VI.

As head of the mistress brigade, Rosa Vanozza had four love children with this power pope and still kept her slim figure. Rosa was thirty when she and Rodrigo began their ten-year dance between the sheets. It's said she had her portrait painted over the door to Alex's bedroom—with Rosa as the Virgin Mary! (Even our century's Madonna would be hard pressed to top that outrageous combination of the sacrilegious and the salacious.)

Rosa outlived husbands, lovers, popes, and some of her offspring, spending her golden years among the taverns and vineyards in which she had so prudently invested. In her sixties, she took up prayer and started rolling over her money and jewels into churches and hospitals; by the time she died at 76, her late-breaking piety earned Rosa a prodigious funeral, full of pomp and followed by two hundred years of pre-paid Masses said in her honor.

*Rosa's main squeeze: a
devilish pope*

Crusades & Pilgrimages, Here We Come

Anna Comnena

A royal whiz kid who lived in the beautiful Byzantine city of Constantinople at the time of the First Crusade, Anna Comnena became a writer and wrote on psychosomatic disease. Among her examples was the connection she saw between envy and gangrene—interesting choice, since Anna herself could have been the first gangrene poster girl. Envy is too pale a word for the lifelong resentment she felt—and wrote about—endlessly.

Here's why: *Porphyrogenitus* or "born to the purple," Princess Anna got engaged at the tender age of eight to the heir apparent. Clear sailing ahead? So it would seem—until along came that horror of medieval times, a royal baby brother, who was apparently replacing her honey as the heir. Worse yet, Anna's young husband-to-be died, leaving her a nine-year-old fiancee in mourning.

Meanwhile, Anna's father, Emperor Alexius, who saw that his beloved daughter was no slouch in the brains department, made sure she got a brilliant education, studying astronomy, medicine, history, military affairs, music, geography, math, and literature from the holy scriptures to the classical authors. This learning was to serve Anna well.

In 1096, the First Crusade, which flooded Constantinople with thousands of armed troops, freelance fanatics, and unarmed pilgrims, brought with it an urgent need for expanded medical facilities. The emperor built a 10,000-bed hospital/orphanage; Anna became its administrator. (Some claim she got in a little hands-on doctoring as well.) Because daddy suffered from gout, she began studying and writing on medical matters.

The princess didn't know it then, but she would most be remembered for her book, *The Alexiad*. Besides lavishing praise on her pop, Anna covered the comings and goings of the crusaders (or "Franks" as the Byzantines called them)—perhaps the only female eye-witness account we still have of those tumultuous events. Her words make us realize that the Crusades weren't just a boy thing: "Full of ardor and enthusiasm, they thronged every highway; and with these warriors came a host of civilians, outnumbering the grains of sand on the seashore, carrying palms in their hands and bearing crosses on their shoulders. There were women and children too, who had left their own countries. Like tributaries joining a river, they streamed from all directions toward us."

Author Comnena unblinkingly reported on everything from the tactical use of flamethrowers on her father's ships to the atrocities (including baby roasting and cannibalism) reportedly committed by the crusaders when they recaptured the city of Nicaea for good ole Byzantium.

Despite her considerable achievements, Anna felt cheated and kept trying to become empress one way or another. Although she improved her position in the next-of-kin sweepstakes by marrying and producing two sons, she never got into the semifinals with dad. Gotta say one thing: She wasn't a quitter. Even after her father's death in 1118, she tried every trick in the book to grab the throne for her hubby—including two conspiracies to put her brother, the brand-new emperor, on ice permanently. To no avail.

Busted for her role in the would-be coups, Anna grumped all the way into the convent, where she had (every writer's fantasy!) the next thirty-five years to polish her manuscript and her most vicious *bons mots* at leisure.

Elizabeth Quintin

Where there's a shrine, there's a gold mine, believed Elizabeth Quintin, a Frenchwoman whose success at retailing roadside religious artifacts paralleled the most popular pastime of the Middle Ages: going on religious pilgrimage. Europe was covered with shrines, connected via major pilgrimage routes, which the Catholic faithful followed. Any excuse sufficed for a circuit: an exercise in faith, adventure—even penance for felony crimes! There being no bumper stickers, tee-shirts, or Kodak moments yet, pilgrims bought badges of the shrines they'd visited to prove to neighbors, priests, parole officers, and other doubting Thomases back home that they'd been there. Each shrine boasted a distinctive badge; famed St. James of Compostela, Spain, for instance, used a scallop shell symbol. Not just any freelance grifter could sell the emblems that pilgrims sewed onto their clothing. As holder of the coveted badge concession at the Le Puy Cathedral, Liz gleefully found that faith *did* move mountains (of badges, at least)—enough to make her a wealthy woman.

Zubayda

Aaron the Upright, grandson of Mohammed the Prophet, knew a good thing when he saw it: his kissin' cousin Zubayda, whom he promptly made his wife. When Aaron became first caliph of Baghdad, Zubayda put together a court whose style would be captured on paper a century later in *The Arabian Nights*. This glamour guru presided in jewel-studded shoes, served rarities such as iced melon delivered on foot from Persia, and staged cast-of-thousands extravaganzas and floating concerts on the Tigris River. Zubayda also kept a few bucks tucked under her magic carpet for worthy purposes. She repaired roads, put in an aqueduct, dug roadside wells, and put up hostels—all to improve the 900-mile pilgrim route between Baghdad and the holy city of Mecca in Arabia. (Just as Christians went on frequent pilgrimages, every devout Moslem sought to visit Mecca—the pilgrimage or *hajj* being one of the five tenets of Islam.) Zubayda also rebuilt Moslem cities and built an aqueduct in Mecca itself. In 792, her own son became caliph. Fond mom barely had time to plan her swearing-in outfit when he was murdered in a succession dustup. Generous-minded to the last, Zubayda refused to revenge her son and in so doing kept her country from civil war.

Spray of Pearls

ed by France's inept King Louie IX, Crusader armies headed for Egypt in 1249 to see what the pickings were, infidel-wise. On the other side, things looked grim in the Egyptian commander-in-chief's tent—the sultan had just expired. As luck would have it, the sultan's wife (or concubine, depending on whose account you believe) happened to be bivouacking with her man. Although her poetic name, Shajar al Durr or "Spray of Pearls," would seem to indicate otherwise, Shajar was made of tough stuff.

She kept mum about the sultan's demise, issuing regular bulletins each day about his "continuing recovery" to the troops and firing off new orders "signed" by the Big Guy. Her major challenge was the unrefrigerated corpse, of course, but this ingenious Egyptian rose to the occasion and held the situation (if not the decomposing cadaver) together.

Under her hidden leadership, the Egyptian troops bravely faced the Crusader armies and soon cut off their supply routes. Plagued with both dysentery and starvation, Louie's troops beat an ignominious retreat. (With this palate of pungent

battlefield aromas, small wonder nobody noticed one paltry rotting body—for whom Shajar hastily held a funeral with appropriate honors, once the Crusaders were up the road.)

In 1250, the Sultan's son and heir, Turan, showed up, ready to be named the next Big Guy. He was promptly killed by the pro-Spray of Pearls faction. Over the next seven years, Shajar stayed on top—but just barely. She got a lot of static, particularly from foreign leaders. Syria's top dog thought women had no place in government. The head honcho in Baghdad was miffed, because he'd originally sent Spray of Pearls as a "from my harem to your harem" gift to the late sultan, and it just didn't seem right for the gift to, you know, do more than look decorative.

To quiet the clamor, the exasperated Sultana Shajar finally married a high military official so he could become sultan. By 1257, she'd had it with married life. She liquidated her new husband, an action that unhappily provoked a parallel reaction. Spray of Pearls was forced to jump off the citadel of Cairo into a ditch without benefit of parachute—a low end for a high-flying woman of power.

Marie Valence

Canny Marie Valence must have been thinking of the old adage, "An army travels on its stomach," when she got the news that the Seventh Crusade was about to blast off from Europe in 1248. After all, when thousands of knights, pilgrims, and other tag-alongs are on the move, they gotta eat. Marie lived in Marseille, a French port that tried to corral all of the Crusader business for a few important retailers by forbidding ships to buy provisions from anyone else. Marie and her business partner neatly got around this restraint of trade by setting up an offshore butchers' emporium on an island in the bay, a mere soupbone's throw from the city. At Marie's offshore oasis, ships could take on animal protein and other provisions. Without a doubt, this French duo did better as butchers than the Crusaders did on their quest; although plenty of human butchery did take place, Crusade Number Seven was a spiritual and tactical flop.

Catherine of Siena

In the Middle Ages, the Christian church tried to clean up pagan fascination with *fascinum,* or penis worship. It didn't succeed. By Catherine of Siena's day in 1350, hundreds of churches bragged about owning Christ's foreskin (or part of it anyway) as a holy relic.

Catherine went them one better. Her own claim? Jesus had given his holy foreskin to *her* as a wedding ring! (I guess diamonds weren't a girl's best friend just yet.) With this statement, this Italian visionary and member of the Dominican Sisters of Penance, a lay order active in the community, had a huge following in no time at all. Lots of devotees were female—no coincidence, since aspiring mothers in medieval times believed that the holy foreskin was a sure-fire fertility charm.

Although they did get underfoot a bit, her religious groupies, called "Caterinati," proved invaluable as *ad hoc* secretaries. A self-taught reader, Catherine had never learned to write, but she had plenty of things she wanted to say. The Caterinati took down hundreds of letters dictated by their "sweet holy mother," as they called her, which were fired off to world leaders from popes to princesses.

Her goals were far-reaching: to make peace between Florence and the pope, and to make war on the infidels by getting another Crusade going. She was also seriously upset at the dual popes in Rome and Avignon, France. (A religious schism had created this rivalry, which didn't get settled for centuries.) In 1376, Catherine succeeded in getting Pope Gregory XI, whom she called "sweetest Babbo mine," to close the Avignon branch—albeit only temporarily. Two years later, he died, and the dueling papacy began anew.

Popes being popes, Catherine's work in the secular world might have done more lasting good. During the bouts of Black Death that raked their way across Europe, she and her band of followers nursed plague victims, later burying the blackened bodies with their own hands.

Born Caterina Benincasa to parents who'd already had twenty-two kids, she got a head-start on guilt, imbibing some of it with her mother's milk. A twin, she was the one who got nursed; her weaker twin, Giovanna, was farmed out to a wet-nurse and died. In her later teachings and writings, Catherine often used the image of nursing from the breast of Christ. Today, this fixation with food and matters mammary might be termed *neurotic*. In Catherine's time, however, her fasting, preparing food for the poor and sick (sometimes at odd hours of the night), and her struggles to overcome normal appetite by eating filth were admired and imitated.

This gentle blond woman barely lived thirty years. You and I might call it a miracle she lasted that long, considering the fasting, whipping, and other physical mortifications she put her body through. She flagellated herself three times a day—once for the Father, once for the Son, and once for the Holy Ghost. At a certain point, she gave up food entirely, merely chewing on bitter herbs and drinking water—later vomiting them up. Some detractors contended her anorexia was insane or possibly demonic. As a result, she was closely observed by the Inquisition, and given a special confessor to monitor her. However, Catherine's manifest sincerity, courage, and radical holiness saved her—and led to her eventual sainthood. As she once said: "*Vidi arcana Dei*—I've seen the hidden things of God."

> "*We are put here in this life like a battlefield and we must fight the good fight.*"
>
> —*Dialogue with Divine Providence*

Celie Rebbe Amelakens

It took a well-known moneychanger named Celie Rebbe Amelakens and her quarrelsome progeny to put the "dys" in dysfunctional family—and it happened way back in fourteenth-century Belgium.

From a family of fishmongers in Ghent, Celie ran her own marine marketplace for several years before jumping several notches up the food chain to become a professional moneychanger. As such, her job involved many of the functions carried out by banks today.

After her marriage to an older man, this working mom had four kids, who soon proceeded to clog up the Belgian court calendars with offenses large and small. In 1353, Jan, the oldest son, killed a certain Pete Taffymaker, then took off for parts unknown. Mom and Pop had to atone for the death by paying "the blood price," as it was called.

Medieval law and order was big on atonement, victim cash payments, physical punishment (e.g., torture, maiming), and religious pilgrimages. In Celie's day, even killers rarely went to jail, because there were very few lockups. Even on foot, an unsupervised three- to six-month trip to Jerusalem or Rome might seem like a wimpy deterrent to our minds, but who knows—maybe the rigors of the journey and the religious cleansing expected at the shrine destinations had more impact than youth offender facilities.

Consequently, when Celie's boys and their cousin got charged with other assaults, off they went on pilgrimages. Over the next twelve years, those rotten little recidivists spent more time on the road than at home. In between assault charges, the boys stood surety (bond, we would call it) several times for homicide. (The homicides weren't always theirs; however, the people asked to stand surety were always accessories or had complicity in the crime.)

For her part, valiant Mrs. Amelakens worked hard, invested in real estate, made money (ever more necessary as she became a widow *and* her sons continued to explore the aggressive sides of their natures), and tried to make the best of it.

It became a mother's nightmare, trying to figure out which relative to rely on. Despite his shaky record of violence and work nonattendance, she finally made her son Jacob a partner in her moneychanging business. Bad move: Soon she was at odds almost continuously with him, as with older son Jan, who became a wine merchant.

When she wasn't worried sick about filial criminal activity and packing lunches for endless pilgrimages, Celie regularly appeared in court to deal with lawsuits and countersuits filed by her nieces, nephews, and in-laws (and by the widow herself, it must be added). The files of this litigation-loving, much put-upon entrepreneur still take up volumes of space in the Ghent city records.

Even after her death, Celie couldn't get any rest, with her kids continuing to squabble over her inheritance. In the final act, Jacob—who probably takes the blue ribbon as the son most despised by the entire family—ended up with the business she'd worked twenty-six years to build. Celie should have stuck to fishier business.

Crusader Washerwomen

arfare never was a males-only activity; in medieval times, for instance, washerwomen were critical factors in the felicity of Crusader armies. After each major battle, the first thing each side would do was ransom its corps of captive laundresses. Even when other female camp followers (prostitutes, nurses, girlfriends, cooks, and so on) got left behind, the army always had its contingent of unsung socks-washers.

Why on earth were these sudsy noncombatants so important? The *D* word, my dear: delousing. At home, men could usually find an accommodating wife or girlfriend to groom them. On campaign, however, wearing thirty to sixty pounds of armor padded with felt, far from bathing facilities (not that medieval Europeans were that keen on showers anyway), sweating like pigs—life was painfully itchy. Body parasites and infection were bigger enemies than the infidels. As British historian Christopher Tyerman once said, "Washerwomen made the lives of the Crusaders less hellish (and less apt to be cut short by disease) by regularly delousing them."

By 1187, the short-term gains of the prior two Crusades had been lost. As everyone knew, this couldn't be the Almighty's fault; it must be due to lack of human diligence or piety.

For the Third Crusade, therefore, the religious organizers and kingly leaders issued an official position paper which said: "This time, the Crusade really *is* going to be a holy war—no women allowed! Except for washerwomen, of course, who will not be a burden nor an occasion for sin."

In 1192, with the Crusaders having failed to take Jerusalem, King Richard the Lion-Hearted and his opponent, Arab leader Saladin, struggled to arrive at a face-saving peace treaty. One of the bargaining chips may have been the fluff-and-fold issue; the Crusaders may have lost, but until they got their own antivermin crew back safe and sound, they weren't about to retreat.

Despite the voluminous writings about the Crusades, you'll look in vain to find a roll call of the intrepid females who meant so much to the men in battle. Like other achievements of a humbler sort, history's great gal groomers did their picking and packing in anonymity—all the more reason for us to honor them.

Agnes Fingerin

Talk about leaving a legacy—there weren't any flies on Agnes Fingerin, a wealthy and highly successful merchant and widow who plied the textile trade in her hometown of Gorlitz, Germany. After amassing a fortune on her own, she paid a lump sum to the municipal tax-collectors toward her future taxes. She specified that the interest from that fund was earmarked for local hospitals, guaranteeing them an annual income. Agnes gave back to the community in other ways, too. In 1471, she set up a fund that provided bread (called *Agnetenbrot* or "Agnes bread" in her honor) to the poor. This was a woman who knew how to invest; 500 years later, her legacy was still putting Agnes bread in the mouths of hungry Gorlitzites. Somehow Agnes Fingerin also found time to travel—which she worked as hard at as she did at business. Among other journeys, she did a round-trip pilgrimage from the country roads of Germany to Jerusalem and the Holy Land—on horseback.

Eleanor of Aquitaine

Throwing on some revealing gilded armor, rounding up a few thousand vassals and a couple of high-society girlfriends in matching outfits, and riding off to the Crusades was just another lark for Eleanor of Aquitaine, easily the most glamorous household name around Europe in the twelfth century. Even given the fact she lived to be eighty-three, she crammed in an amazing amount of accomplishment and adventure.

To start with, she ruled as queen of France for fifteen years and queen of England for fifty more, producing ten kids when she wasn't busy with music, health care, or political maneuverings.

A jet-setter 900 years before jets, Eleanor couldn't do just one thing at a time. While making her way to Jerusalem with husband King Louis on the Second Crusade, for instance, she noticed the carnage en route and founded a few hospitals to help out. That done, they moved on to Antioch, where Eleanor flirted with her uncle Raymond and other fun-loving royals of Syria. Damp-blanket Louie, meanwhile, shaved off his hair and beard—which moved the queen to say, "That chin is grounds for a divorce." Their marriage, which had produced two daughters, was eventually annulled; the Second Crusade, a major embarrassment despite Eleanor's contributions, *should* have been annulled also.

Now thirty, the new divorcee quickly wed nineteen-year-old Henry II, soon to be king of England. Was it real love this time? More like real *estate:* Their combined holdings included England and more than half of France—which really put a certain ex-husband's nose out of joint, as did Eleanor's ability to crank out male heirs with Henry. Soon there were eight little Plantagenets running around. This marriage turned out to be no bed of roses either, as Eleanor watched Henry get fatter and more faithless.

In 1170, royally fed up with the philandering Plantagenet, she and daughter Marie turned their courts in France and England into troubadour-filled "courts of love," built around the premise that "true love is a game for single people."

Passion might be fun and games, but Eleanor evidently found politics and war games more to her liking. At age fifty, she and two of her sons led her Aquitaine army against Henry. The king took it in double overtime and left the queen to spend her next fifteen years in jail. (Well, house arrest in one drafty castle after another—no day at the beach, anyway.)

Once Henry died in 1189, Eleanor got out of lockup, and her favorite son Richard took the throne. Leaving Eleanor in charge of England, Ricky soon left for the Third Crusade, where Mr. Lion-Hearted managed to lose 95,000 out of 100,000 troops and get captured as well. Thanks to his ghastly performance, no one cared to raise his ransom. After Richard languished in a Vienna prison for two years, good ole mom had to step in, write hate letters to the pope, and hustle the 130,000-mark ransom herself.

Although she'd never been keen on her youngest son Johnny (Henry's pet), Eleanor got him out of hot water, too, when he in turn became king of England. Nearly eighty when a rebellion against John flared up, she left her fireside, threw on her by-now deplorably unstylish armor, and led her own army to crush the opposition. A classy, take-no-crap, Katherine Hepburn of a woman whose zest for life never wore out, wouldn't you say? In a neat case of art imitating life, Hepburn herself won an Academy Award in 1968 for playing Eleanor of Aquitaine in that memorable and semi-accurate film, *The Lion in Winter*.

Female Troubadours

Lacking boom boxes, music *aficionadas* like Queen Eleanor of Aquitaine (whose granddaddy was the first troubadour of note) enjoyed their music live. With her clout as queen of France and later England, Eleanor's enthusiasm propelled troubadours into the musical celebrities of her day. As it turns out, there were women among them, too, lamenting the rocky road to courtly love and throwing out pert suggestions as to where somebody could stuff their cheatin' hearts. They were called *trobaritz*—the Provençal word for female troubadours, and it took brass for these women to get out and perform. In fact, many began as wealthy patrons of male troubadours, later taking the leap into participation and/or composing. A northern Frenchwoman who called herself "Marie of France" (thought to be a stage name for a royal in-law of Eleanor's) had hit after hit as a minstrel in the English court. No three-minute airplay here; Marie's "Lais" and other romances ran hundreds of lines. During her life, Marie's musical work—which daringly called for women to take the initiative in love-making—went international, getting translated into Norse, Middle English, and High German.

Most *trobaritz* came from southern France—songwriter-patron Maria de Ventadorn, for example, who married into a long line of tune-carrying bluebloods and performed at Eleanor's court as well as her own. So far, only one of her songs has been found; in it, she advocates love relationships that even the most uppity woman of modern times could get behind. ". . . the lady ought to do exactly for her lover/as he does for her, without regard to rank; for between two friends neither one should rule."

The Countess of Dia took a different tack. In one of her four surviving songs, she wrote lyrics as bittersweet and modern as Carly Simon: "With me you always act so cold, but with everyone else you're so charming." There were also female troubadours who openly expressed their earthy love for other women, such as the song by Beatritz de Romans, an outrageous ballad to a certain Maria.

Although our biographical information on these women (at least fifteen are known by name) is in tatters, fortune has left at least some of their music and lyrics, whose melodic charms can be heard on CDs—and on occasion, live—just as Queen Eleanor would have liked it.

You go, girl: 12th-century trobaritz rock Europe

Melissande

You'd think that when the crusaders managed to seize the holy city of Jerusalem that they'd run the place in a civilized way. You'd be terribly disappointed. And it wasn't only men who made mischief. Queen Melissande, for example, who got to boss Jerusalem between 1131 and 1152, was every bit as talented at breaking the Golden Rule and the Ten Commandments as any of her male counterparts.

While her parents, Queen Morphia (yep!) and King Baldwin, fretted over finding their queen-to-be daughter the right husband, Mel carried on a smoking romance with a good-looking guy named Hugh, an aristocrat so minor he wasn't even in the semifinals, consort-wise.

The parents' choice? A French count called Fulk V of Anjou. Mom and Dad threw the fanciest wedding in Christendom for Mel, who remained in a royal snit because Fulk was 1) too short, 2) too old, and 3) had a complexion that would make a gravel road look good. Hugh Studmuffin was in a similar funk, having meanwhile married an affluent widow with grown kids.

Even after Melissande became Queen of Jerusalem, Hugh and Mel kept on commiserating with each other, if you know what I mean. Both Fulk and Hugh's wife being jealous types, the whole situation blew up. In a very short period, Jerusalem saw a duel, a botched assassination, and a very public execution in which poor Hugh was hacked to death. This time Queen Mel's sulk lasted for years.

About 1143, her mood brightened, when King Fulk got a fatal bashing after being bucked off horseback. Solo rule, that's the ticket.

She was truly in her glory a few years later, when the glitterati of the Second

Crusade hit the Holy Land. (She'd almost given up on them—it had been years since she'd sent a "Jerusalem's in trouble—send crusaders" letter with a genuine sliver of the True Cross in it.) Now here they were. Strolling arm-in-arm with Queen Eleanor of Aquitaine, making cocktail chatter with two German kings and Eleanor's spouse, French King Louie, Mel found herself hostessing the Grand Fromages of European nobility.

Melissande's reception didn't disappoint. The crusaders—especially the women, who hadn't seen a decent dwelling or any moisturizer for months—thought they'd entered Christian heaven. After living in drafty, dog-filled, dark European castles, Mel's swell stuff, from Oriental carpets to mosaics and silk sheets, really impressed them. Naturally, Mel subjected them to a tour of her building projects—from the covered market to the Abbey of St. Lazarus.

Things were a lot duller around Jerusalem when company left, only livening up when Mel's son Baldwin got old enough to want to run the kingdom. Just to make him happy, Mel said, "Okay, we'll throw a big party—make it a mom and son coronation." Spiteful Baldwin muttered okay. On the sly, however, the twenty-two year old changed the date of the coronation and got crowned earlier without her.

The ensuing knock-down, drag-out went on for years until mom and son finally did the mature thing: split their holy land real estate in half. Eventually tired of feuding, Melissande entered the medieval equivalent of a rest home: a convent she'd founded at Bethany. From there, it was just five minutes to her digs for all eternity—the Tomb of the Virgin, in the Valley of Jehoshaphat—a truly ironic choice, given Mel's track record.

Eglentyne

Lovers of Chaucer's *Canterbury Tales* may think that the characters in his fourteenth-century classic are fiction. Not the Prioress anyway, who's based on Madame Eglentyne, the flesh-and-blood female head of an English nunnery. (Voluminous church records about her life and antics still exist.)

Like countless other medieval children, Eglentyne had no say-so about her entrance into the religious life. After paying a stiff dowry fee, her dad plunked his little girl into the nunnery, where she grew up learning to sing, read, speak French, and sew.

Turns out that gray-eyed Eglentyne had what it took to become prioress or head of the convent: a sweet disposition, upper-class connections, and nice table manners. At least, that's what counted with the nuns who voted her in when the old prioress died. The nunnery being a business and farm as well as a religious institution, Eglentyne as its head was supposed to keep the books straight and the convent in the black. She wasn't awfully good at it. Luckily, the bishop understood her math phobia and worked around it.

Where Eglentyne ran into religious hot water were the four Ds, also known as the nuns' downfall: dress, dogs, dances, and those demonic pilgrimages. Nuns had a dress code—cover it up and make it black. Eglentyne, however, didn't see what harm could come from a few gold rings and hairpins, a silver girdle, a two-foot hennin headdress, and some furs. Okay, and maybe a lowcut dress with a train for special occasions. Even more distressing, she wore her veil hitched up, letting the world get a gander at her totally nude forehead. (High bare brows were a fashion must in her day—except for nuns, who were expected to cover their brows with a wimple.)

Pets in the convent were another no-no: "bad for discipline," the bishops said.

Eglentyne, it must be admitted, had a pooch or two. Still, she could point to another prioress who got away with keeping a pack of dogs *and* a monkey in her room.

But the most outrageous thing Prioress Eglentyne did (and that nuns continued to do, and that bishops continued to forbid, for six centuries) was "wandering in the world." That elastic phrase meant anything from short shopping trips to town to gallivanting about the English countryside in Canterbury-style pilgrimages. Eglentyne, who traveled with another nun and three priests, chalked up more "business travel" mileage than half the bishops. (Of course, travel for male church officials was totally acceptable.)

Since 791, the clergy had been thundering at religious women to stay put. Bishops tried to get Eglentyne and the rest of them to obey this injunction for centuries, right up until 1545. That was the moment when every nunnery in England was dissolved by King Henry VIII—at which point all English nuns got turned out to wander in the secular world, like it or not.

So make the doorways bigger!

Margery Kempe & Julian of Norwich

On one hand, most of the folks Margery Kempe ran across would rather be horsewhipped than spend much time in her presence, what with her religious exhortations, haranguings for higher levels of purity, and floods of tears, to say nothing of her fainting fits, shrieks, and roars. Restful, Margery was not. Nevertheless, this middle-class English mayor's daughter who never learned to read or write led an extraordinary life.

Or more accurately, two lives. As a teen, Margery committed a sin that doomed her to an infinity in hell. Or so she thought. After marriage and the birth of her first child, she tried to confess and failed; belief in her damned state led to a mental breakdown, followed by a direct-from-God religious experience in which she was forgiven. Margery bounced back, buying fashionable clothes again, lustily enjoying her husband John, and having thirteen more kids.

The new duds and more mouths to feed added up; Margery started a brewery to increase cash flow. Hard to believe in beer-swilling Britain, but it failed, as did her miller enterprise. John had his hands full dealing with Mrs. K., and eventually gave up working altogether.

Then Mrs. Kempe got the notion to become a roving proseletizer for the Lord, her own religious channel, as it were. Her traveling evangelist career was part of the Beguine movement, a nonconvent religious way of life that swept across Europe. Margery, however, aspired to be a freelance holy woman. To avoid the highly inflammable label of heretic, she needed references—so she buttonholed Julian, England's top anchoress or religious recluse. A cheerful mystic who'd written *Revelations of Divine Love* from her tiny cell, Julian believed in a loving God and a simple life praising Him. No revelations, however, could have prepared the seventy-year-old sage for garrulous Marge, who babbled until she squeezed a testimonial out of Julian.

By this time, Marge was having misgivings about sex and talked her husband into a legal separation—to allow them both to achieve spiritual bliss.

That done, she embarked on her greatest adventure: a pilgrimage to the Holy Land. During the first months of the journey, Kempe enraged and irritated her fellow pilgrims so much with her hysterics and preaching that they returned the money she'd paid to be part of the group and ran off. The unsinkable Kempe managed to get over the Alps with an old man as a guide and bandit-foiler. In Venice, the group ended up in the same Palestine-bound boat with Margery, where she and her sorely-tried companions landed in 1414.

Christian pilgrims to Jerusalem had a tendency to sing, sob, kiss the holy places, and otherwise emote—but nobody topped Mrs. K.'s performance at the church of the Holy Sepulchre. Moving from altar to altar, she went into convulsions, emitted extraordinary screams, and had vivid visions of Christ bleeding, which she described to the awed and half-deafened crowd.

Her place secure in paradise, Mrs. Kempe made an eventful return to England, followed by other pilgrimages to Spain and Norway. In her sixties, she hired a scribe to pen her memoirs, in which Kempe referred to herself as "this creatur." Unlucky in her hiring policies, Marge found the ghostwriter's mangled English and German unintelligible, requiring two more scribes to finish the book. That editorial nightmare, however, was nothing compared to the time it took to get the book in print. A mere 503 years after her hotly emotional words were put to paper, the *Book of Margery Kempe* came off the press—giving us a tangy look at a world by turns religious, raucous, and ripely real.

Joan of Arc

Few female teens in history have gotten the ink Joan of Arc has. Fewer still have gotten it by being *good*. Joan was brave as well as good; this French shepherd could have cornered the "No fear" tee-shirt concession in a Paris minute.

At thirteen, she heard heavenly voices that foretold she would help weak King Charles VII fight the English and liberate the besieged city of Orleans. Within three years, she'd lobbied the powerful women around the king, gotten Charles to give her an army, and was leading 4,000 enthusiastic troops in a high-gloss suit of armor that any self-respecting televangelist would sin for. On April 28, 1429, Joan freed Orleans; by summer, the English army was history, and Charles got crowned at Rheims.

She battled armies, inquisitioners and— mon Dieu! tax collectors

Besides making sure her relatives had good seats for the coronation, the king asked Ms. de Arc to name her reward. This altruistic miss said, "How about lowering the taxes for Domremy (her home town) and Greux?" The surprised monarch complied; for centuries the two towns got tax bills marked "No balance due."

Hundred-year wars are like showbiz— you're only as good as your last triumph. After Joan flopped at taking Paris for Charles, the English nabbed her and the French king did nothing. At her heresy/witchcraft trial, her accusers cited such "occult" behavior as wearing men's clothes. On May 30, 1431, the Maid of Orleans, nineteen and still a virgin (although the English tried hard to change that while she was imprisoned), was burned at the stake, dying with amazing grace. Her secret weapon? Belief in God and the role she was destined to play in her country's deliverance. Twenty years later, the king overturned the guilty verdict, awarding her family pensions and honors; a mere five hundred years later, the gallant teen herself was declared a saint.

> *"Children say that people are hanged sometimes for speaking the truth."*
>
> —spoken at her trial,
> February 23, 1431

Joan of Arc Wanna-bes

The "just do it" life of martyr and heroine Joan of Arc in fifteenth-century France attracted any number of suicidally devout wanna-bes, most of whom called themselves Joan (Jeanne in French) to enhance the likeness. Among the crowd: Jeanne La Férone of Le Mans, a camp follower who asserted she could cure ulcers, prophesize, and lead armies. When her brag of being a virgin proved incorrect, La Férone's other claims were challenged, and she was sentenced to tour the town in a dunce cap.

Another copycat was the Maid of Sarmaize, a Joan who bummed around dressed in male clothing, preaching and hitting on the real Joan's friends and relatives for acceptance (or failing that, food and lodging). A third voice-guided contender named Pierronne was said to have fought in the French army; like her heroine, young Ms. P. was condemned to be burnt at the stake.

Jeanne des Armoises, the most genuine of the Joan wanna-bes, was a mother with two kids. For two years, she fought for France with such distinction she was given command of numerous soldiers. This Jeanne also got reprimanded for hymenal shortfall, to which she replied: "My value is not dependent on virginity." Despite valor and quick wit, Jeanne ended up in irons and had to declare herself an official Joan of Arc imposter in 1440. She, however, may have escaped a high-Fahrenheit fate. A surviving document from an inquisitor of the 1440s talks regretfully about "the one who got away"—a Joan reincarnation who escaped being burned alive. In those brutal witch-panicky times, that counted as a major accomplishment.

Persecution Mania, Witch-buring Madness

Gracia Mendes Nasi

In Yiddish, there's a saying: "God made troubles. Also shoulders." If that's the case, Gracia Mendes must have had a build like a Chicago linebacker. In her day (circa 1510–69), Jews had just gone through four centuries of being slaughtered by crusaders on their way to kill infidels, and being expelled from countries they'd made their own. The all-purpose medieval scapegoats, Jews got blamed for plagues, famines, witchcraft, and not being good Christians.

Is it any wonder then that the first forty years of Gracia's life read like a frequent flyer's passport? Born in Portugal to well-to-do parents, she and her family were called "New Christians" or more typically, *marranos* (pig in Spanish), the epithet for Jews who'd been forced to convert. However, Gracia never jettisoned her Judaism; in fact, when she married Francisco Mendes at 18, she may have wed an undercover rabbi.

The couple built a thriving international business in the spice trade; eight years later, Gracia was left a widow with a young daughter. That same year, the pope ordered a full-on Inquisition in Portugal. Collecting her nephews, sister, daughter, and that critical instrument for flight, her fortune, Gracia hopped around Europe, looking for a place where she could make a life and be Jewish too. They made a pit stop in England (nope), dallied in Antwerp (her money welcome, religion not very), and hung out in Venice (where Gracia got temporarily arrested). When her entourage reached Ferrara, Italy, Gracia thought she'd found her safe haven.

Besides having a business head on her shoulders, this maven of moves was getting a reputation for activism. For instance, she and her brother-in-law brazenly lobbied the pope to stop the Inquisition in Portugal, who was so surprised that he did—for a while. Working the other direction, Gracia set up an underground railroad for Portuguese Jews, whereby hundreds escaped. In Ferrara, Gracia got to openly use her Jewish name of Gracia Mendes Nási for the first time in her life.

Seems like she'd just gotten unpacked when trouble brewed again. This time, however, somebody actually offered her asylum—the Sultan of Turkey, no less. In 1553, a mere 17 years after they fled Portugal, Gracia and family settled in Constantinople, where she became the most influential woman of her day. Besides her philanthropic, business, and banking activities, she had a showdown with yet another pope, who'd been persecuting *marranos* in Italy.

As welcoming as Constantinople was, and as luxuriously and openly as she lived, Gracia gradually came to believe that Palestine was the best place for Jews. Throwing out a feeler, this early Zionist offered a few zillion ducats to the Turks (who happened to own Palestine at that time) to see if she could set up a Jewish settlement in Tiberias on the Sea of Galilee. After consummating the deal, Gracia's community of 60,000 settled on the Galilee shores. In the years before her death, Gracia probably made Tiberias her home also. Although many of the original settlers left after their founder passed away, the nucleus of Gracia's vision is still going strong at the school of Mikveh Israel. Her adoptive home of Turkey hasn't forgotten her, either—synagogues in Izmir and elsewhere still bear her name.

Isabel La Católica

A major prenuptial agreement giving the woman all the cards? *Sí, sí, sí,* as Isabel said to Ferdinand, the mild-mannered second cousin she chose to marry in 1469 in order to unite Spain. Instead of churros and chocolate, this determined young Queen of Castile ate ambition for breakfast. As a teen, she'd already survived banishment, plots, and the intrigues of a slimy half brother and an illegitimate sister, and was adept at gamesmanship, military moves, and the art of private negotiation and public kowtowing to male heads of family (a required course for every Spanish woman).

When she married, Isabel insisted on parity and autonomy. She would run Castile, Ferdie would run Aragon. As a team, they would rule Spain. Instead of agonizing over a china pattern, she picked out a motto to reflect her philosophy: *Tanto monta, monta tanto, Fernando como Isabel, Isabel como Fernando,* meaning "They rule with equal rights and both excel, Isabel as much as Ferdinand, Ferdinand as much as Isabel."

Besides her astonishing power stance as a hands-on queen, Isabel was one amazing horsewoman on the battlefield—which may account for the miscarriages she suffered, including one during the siege of Toledo in 1475. (Nevertheless, between her stints as Amazon, she still did the queen-as-breeder bit and had five kids in fifteen years.)

What with dirty politics, horseback riding, and so forth, Isabel never got a polished education as a kid. In later life, she remedied that by bringing Beatrix Galindo and Francisca de Lebrija, the most celebrated female intellectuals of the day, to her traveling court. Among other subjects, they taught Latin (language of diplomacy and religion) to her and her daughters.

Politically adept, pious, energetic, bright, honest, and globally visionary, Isabel lacked just one quality to qualify for greatness: religious tolerance. A rigid Catholic, in the 1480s she and Fernando began a pricey ten-year war whose sole object was to eject, convert, and/or exterminate the Moors, the gypsies, and the Jews. The duo also put the Inquisition and its thugs into motion, which jump-started the spread of heresy trials, witch hunts, and other human rights disasters throughout Europe.

The queen had her compassionate side. When it came to bullfights, she was (like queasy tourists) for the bull. (At the birth of her son John, she grudgingly allowed one public bullfight.) During the Moor war, she set up the first MASH unit ever seen—a six-tent outfit with over 400 wagons as ambulances.

The accomplishment for which Isabel receives most credit during her 30-year reign is, of course, her underwriting of Christopher Columbus. He hung around the Spanish court for eons, begging for a grant to find a shortcut to "the Indies" (by which he meant the Far East and India), promising spices, gold, and other useful items. The queen and Chris had lots in common: besides mystical beliefs in their God-ordained roles, both were auburn-haired, blue-eyed—and towered over Ferdie. Never keen on the idea, the king let Isabel spend her own money on this crossing-the-ocean notion. (She'd already hocked her best jewels to get the Moors out, so Chris got the cheapest ships going.) When the New World proved unspicy, Isabel put on the pressure for gold. (Chris was a real disappointment in that department.)

Nevertheless, the haul was such that the New World—and Isabel's role in its discovery—had a golden aura, exemplified by coins like the *excellente,* on which Isabel and Ferdie are pictured nose-to-nose. Even on this coin, she stands taller than the king—as she did, literally and figuratively, in real life.

Nicolaea & Alice Samuel

The worst centuries to be female occurred in mid-Renaissance, when the label "witch" meant torture and a 50-50 chance of execution for hundreds of thousands of Europeans. It was a war without borders, a campaign of social control and terror waged mainly against women. While da Vinci painted and Shakespeare wrote, while hundreds of holy women like St Catherine won acclaim, thousands of women got burnt alive.

Many were healers, doing work valued by the community. A French healer named Nicolaea, for instance, who'd learned to be a plague-ridder the hard way—in lieu of a fee, her mentor had raped her. (Nicolaea got the "bonus" of an illegitimate son to raise.) Later, in 1587, her mentor was convicted of being a witch. Soon after, Nicolaea was hired to plague-rid Dommartin castle, carried out the job, and got paid. But then an official's wife became ill. Who you gonna blame? The plague-buster with a witch for a mentor, naturally. Nicolaea and son were imprisoned. Talk about a lose/lose situation—if Nicolaea let the patient die, she'd be blamed and beaten. If she acted, she'd be providing "proof" she was a witch.

As often happened in witch hunts, her son turned on her. Caught trying to escape, he said, "Beat her to get the truth!" They did just that, until Nicolaea finally agreed to treat the invalid. Under her care, the woman got well; at a certain point, mother and son were told they could go. They were almost out the gates of the castle when they were seized by local authorities, locked up, and reinterrogated. At length, Nicolaea lost her fight, saying whatever they wanted to hear. In the fiery final act, mother and son were burnt at the stake together.

Kids played a big role in witch trials—sometimes as victims; mothers, it was believed, passed witchcraft down to their daughters. As a result, toddlers went to prison. Children as young as eight got executed. Mostly, however, in this panicky climate of belief that the devil was using female witches to destroy male-dominated European societies, children became accusers, pressured and/or encouraged to give evidence against adults.

One infamous case involved five English girls, the Throckmorton sisters, who accused Alice Samuel, an elderly villager, of bewitching them—and later, their servants. Today we'd probably label the girls' fits, shrieks, and sneezing attacks as ploys to get attention and avoid homework. In 1592, however, people believed this sort of "evidence" was "proof" of witchcraft. Dreams were "proof" too. Lady Cromwell, a nosy friend of the family, confronted Mrs. Samuel, called her a witch, and cut off a hank of her hair. (Hair-burning was thought to reduce magic powers.) That night, Lady C dreamt a cat tried to tear away her flesh—a feline clearly sent by Alice. Cromwell went on to "prove" Alice's powers by having fits, then dying.

Eventually the sisters convinced Mrs. Samuel she was a witch. Alice even came to believe she'd used six pet chickens to hex the kids and kill Lady Cromwell. This would all be sublimely ridiculous if it hadn't been fatal. At the trial, a jury found Mrs. Samuel (plus her daughter and husband) guilty; they were hanged. Their property was awarded to Lady Cromwell's husband—a windfall that was the motive behind many a witch accusation.

Medieval times ran red with persecutions—against Jews, Moslems, Native Americans, religious heretics. But the witch craze systematically went after women. The scapegoats were neighbors, the herbalist down the block, your own mother. Like other holocausts, the witch craze's major weapon is memory. So remember Nicolaea, and Alice Samuel, and what was done to them, and to a hundred thousand more.

Lady Killigrew

Life as the wife of England's vice admiral of Cornwall could be frightfully ho-hum; Lady Killigrew longed for a career—but what? She was willing to travel, looking for risk-taking opportunities, and wanted to work with people . . . suddenly the Killigrew family tradition of privateering (an upper-crust euphemism for piracy) came to mind. Shiver me timbers—a direct hit! After a few trial runs with her husband, Lady K. soloed one spring night in 1582. Her target: a German ship laden with goodies, anchored in Falmouth Harbor on the south Cornwall coast. With its female captain at the helm, her boat and crew came alongside the vessel.

New manager Killigrew wasn't about to delegate the dirty work, and led the charge with cutlass and pistol to do her murderous share. After tidying the target ship by deep-sixing the victims, she checked out that cargo. More beginner's luck: Her loot included barrels of silver coin, which she and her pirate band managed to row to shore.

Wouldn't you know it, though, Lady Killigrew's career with a bullet was cut short by a royal killjoy—Queen Elizabeth I. Although Liz had been turning a blind eye to English privateering (in hopes of pushing the Spaniards and other Europeans out of her backyard), Killigrew's case was a bit too in-your-face to ignore. With a heavy heart, she decreed that Killigrew had been very naughty. At the trial, this upper-class swashbuckler got a "hang 'em high!" verdict along with her less exalted second mates.

Like a good British mystery, at the eleventh hour the queen rethought her capital punishment decision; Lady

Killigrew got a very long stay in lockup instead. (Given the notorious English damp and the lack of in-cell amenities at the time, our cruelly downsized career woman might have preferred hanging.)

Reyna Nasi

An exceptionally bright Jewish girl, Reyna spent her first twenty years packing and unpacking. So did the rest of her family; headed by redoubtable activist Gracia Mendes Nasi, they wandered throughout Europe, looking for a home where they could just let down their hair and be Jewish in safety. Once the family found a permanent home in Turkey, Reyna dutifully married her cousin, Joseph Nasi, urged on by her high-voltage mama. Joseph became the matriarch's right-hand man, running the family's merchant fleet and other businesses. Only after both her mother and her husband died did Reyna come into her own. She then set up as a printer. For seven years, her presses published books in Hebrew for the Jewish community in Turkey. As one of the few countries that welcomed Jews, you'd better believe that their growing numbers—and their thirst for books—kept Reyna busy and prosperous.

Eufanie Macalyne

Medieval women like Eufanie Macalyne had many up-close-and-painful experiences with childbirth. Prenatal care was, shall we say, in the Dark Ages; hygiene, ditto. A woman might be pregnant dozens of times. So who could blame this Scottish noblewoman for wanting something to ease the agony? At a certain excruciating point in her labor, Eufanie asked her midwife for a wee hit of drugs. Instead of herbal bliss, Eufanie got brought up on witchcraft charges, dragged to the nearest bonfire, and burned alive for her incredible temerity! (Had she delivered at this point? Did the midwife get charged too? The records are silent.) Now if the mother-to-be had asked for a Christian charm around her thigh to ease the pain, she'd have gotten room service in a minute. Anything else, however, was a red-hot capital offense in the Scotland of 1591, which shared with Germany the dubious distinction of carrying out ferocious, large-scale witch hunts and executions.

Erszebet Báthory

Could it be something in that Carpathian mountain water? Those lonely peaks (now part of Romania) were home to Vlad the Impaler, the fearsome figure upon which Count Dracula was based. But Vlad was bush league when it came to Transylvanian Terror. Minutes away as the bat flies, a Hungarian sadist named Erszebet Báthory gave new meaning to the word bloodthirsty. Countess Erszebet had a yen to stay young—and thought daily baths in the blood of young girls would do the trick. There being any number of

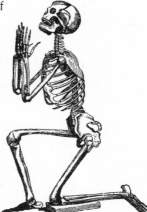

powerless females living in and around her castle, she murdered 610 of them and soaked in their corpuscles for years before anyone caught on. Despite their sluggish deductive powers, locals were finally able to bring the countess to justice; Erszebet had kept a meticulous diary of her sanguinary health regime, which formed the main evidence at her trial in 1611. After a no-surprise "guilty" verdict, the woman who out-Draculaed Dracula on his own turf was walled up in her own castle, where she died (but do we know this *for sure?*) three years later.

Alice Kyteler & Petronilla of Meath

You know the Irish—they've never behaved the way they should, that is, the way the English thought they should. The tale of Alice Kyteler and Petronilla of Meath is a good example of Celtic courage. In the early 1300s, the pope sent an English bishop named Richard Ledrede to Kilkenny. His job: to set up an inquisition, nose around for witches in Ireland, and bring down a woman of standing in the community. Not only would this put the fear of the papacy into the Irish ruling classes—it would put those free-spirited Celtic females in their place.

In 1324, the bishop ran across a person with the perfect victim profile—a wealthy, three-time widow named Dame Alice Kyteler whose fourth husband had gone insane. Even better, some of her children had been heard to whine that they didn't get what they deserved in the various wills left by this string of decedents. Bishop Ledrede, aided by his inquisition staff, well-trained in the arts of threats and torture, took those aggrieved kids into custody. Soon he had them composing a whole list of imaginary crimes: yes, their mother had "without a doubt" killed her husbands; "everyone knew" she'd made a demonic sacrifice of nine roosters and nine peacocks; and "most probably" she was sleeping with a devil named Robin MacArt.

However, Bishop Ledrede barked up the wrong broomstick when he took on Alice. She didn't just dispute the politically motivated charges—she *took* charge. Through her various well-connected family members, she got the bishop arrested and thrown in jail for seventeen days! Wisely, she left Kilkenny at that point and went to live in Dublin. Once he'd gotten sprung, the hornet-mad bishop made his case in front of Catholic officials in Dublin. This round, he won, and Alice fled Ireland for England.

Due to her hasty departure, Mrs. Kyteler had to leave behind her properties and much of her wealth. The vengeful persecutors fell on those left behind—the innocent members of her family and her household. Several of her relatives ended up in prison. The hammer fell hardest on the humble people—in this case, Dame Alice's servants. (Witch hunts often did focus on the most powerless in a community—especially widows or single women without family.) They were whipped through town, excommunicated, or banished.

But Petronilla of Meath, Alice's personal servant, bore the brunt. Flogged six times, ritually tortured, she eventually confessed to being a witch. On November 3, 1324, Petronilla had the mournful distinction of being the first person in Ireland to be burnt at the stake for the heresy of sorcery.

Although Ireland would have very few other witch hunts, the trial of Kyteler and the execution of Petronilla did attract attention throughout Europe, setting precedents (from demonic sex charges to the severity of punishments) for much of what followed.

Eventually Bishop Ledrede was accused of heresy himself—twice. (Nice bit of karma, that.) It's not known if Dame Alice ever got to return to the olde sod. Her home, the oldest in Kilkenny, and now known as Kyteler's Inn, still stands, a 700-year-old monument to female defiance.

Drat! I'm one peacock short for a witchcraft indictment

Margaret Porète

Being a religious mystic could mean painful martyrdom, as an independent Frenchwoman named Margaret Porète found out. A villager from Hainaut, early in life Margaret felt a spiritual pull which led her to enter the ranks of the Beguines.

Although some Beguines lived communally in béguinages throughout France, Germany, and Belgium, they were not part of the Catholic ecclesiastical infrastructure. This women-only religious movement began in the thirteenth century with two motives. Women who wanted to follow Christ by working among the sick and poor thought the nun lifestyle was getting way too soft; Beguines wanted a more useful life. There was also the matter of dowries: it cost a surprising amount of dough to get into a nunnery—any nunnery. There were waiting lists to get in. With the Beguines, you could enter no matter what your economic circumstances.

Since Beguines weren't an official part of the church, bishops and popes alike nervously scrutinized their doings, hoping to catch them drift in doctrinal error—or heresy.

Margaret, whose only failing seemed to be a hardheaded refusal to do things the Church's way, carried out a lot of community work, preached publicly, translated the Bible into French, and opted to live in secular society instead of bunking at the nearest béguinage. That was bad enough, but she *really* got her wimple in a wringer after she wrote a mystical work called *The Mirror of Simple Souls,* which circulated throughout France.

In it, she wrote that for a soul to reach communion with God, it had to work through seven levels of divine grace. At level six, the soul resembled an angel,

Margaret said, an angel with no need for sermons, sacraments, or the Church. At least in aghast officials' minds, that set off the old heresy alarm, and Margaret got hauled into court.

Stubborn author that she was, Ms. Porète refused to defend herself, answer questions, or get a Parisian lawyer. After all, her hardcover carried the warning, "This book is not for everyone," as well as her statement that salvation could also be reached by traditional church means.

Her 1310 trial was a travesty. Her judges really knew how to hurt a writer—they hadn't even read her book. Led by a team of crack inquisitors, the prosecution helpfully copied off a few out-of-context sections as crib notes for the judges. This being

an era of high tension in France, with numerous people being brought to trial for witchcraft and political heresy alike, Margaret's verdict of "guilty of heretical mysticism" came as no shock.

She stoutly went to her death by burning at the stake, still believing in her own words. What's more, other readers did too—and continued to do so. Numerous copies of her book survived in monastery libraries around Europe. Eventually, *Mirror of Simple Souls* came to be so well thought of that credit for its authorship was later laid at the door of a fifteenth-century Flemish mystic—a guy named Jan.

Benedetta Carlini & Bartolomea Crivelli

A *bambina* of nine when she entered the humblest nunnery in Pescia, Benedetta Carlini became its youngest abbess—and no wonder. Besides management skills and cajoling talents that kept the convent's cash flow positive, she had divine gifts as a mystic. Benedetta predicted the future—that a plague would hit Pescia in 1631, for instance. She had long conversations with male angels. Her forehead and hands regularly bled—a phenomenon called stigmata. She went into trances on command. Eventually she reported that she had exchanged hearts with Jesus. Later, she married Christ in a special ceremony attended by a few select guests. The abbess, however, really pushed the spiritual envelope when she foretold her own death, "died," and returned with orders for her nuns along the lines of, "I can get you into Paradise . . . probably . . . if you do exactly as I say."

In 1622, the church sent officials to investigate Benedetta's showy claims. During the course of the investigation, their interviews turned up more surprising tid-bits: The abbess had an almost demonic craving for Italian salami, one nun tattled. The abbess helped along her stigmata with a large needle, another keyhole-peeper reported. But the biggest headline-grabber was the news that sister Benedetta had a sex life as intense and splashy as her spiritual and temporal ones. Nun Bartolomea

Crivelli revealed that she and the abbess had had a two-year, three-times-a-week affair—not that *she* liked it, the young canary hastily added.

In medieval Europe, lesbian sexuality didn't exist (at least in the minds of males). To describe the acts that took place between the lusty abbess and little Bart, the horrified clergy resorted to phrases like "mutual corruption." (During the juicier bits, the scribe taking it down got so shaken that his calligraphy became almost illegible!)

When confronted with Bart's story, the nimble-tongued abbess gave a Reaganesque response: "I have no recollection—it musta been that angel Splenditello." Indeed, Bart and others said that when the abbess hit her stride with an angelic vision, her voice deepened and her face took on the expression of a male teen. Psychologically this made sense; becoming a horny "male angel" allowed Benedetta to create an identity that fit into—and made an end run around—the values of her patriarchal society.

After wrenching thought, church investigators gave the abbess a break: She'd evidently been possessed by the devil and thus wasn't fully accountable for her actions. (Unlike witchcraft, possession was considered "involuntary.") Instead of a date with a bonfire, Benedetta got locked into a convent cell for thirty-five years. Evidently perceived as the innocent victim in the situation, Bartolomea, the young squealer, remained a nun at Pescia.

Although neither nuns nor locals protested her harsh treatment, Benedetta kept her standing as a visionary—especially after she hit the mark with the plague prediction. At her death, Benedetta scored a final posthumous triumph. Unconcerned about her sex life, faithful fans flocked to the chapel, to touch her body, or better yet, to try and steal a relic from the holy woman they thought of as a confidant of angels.

The Joys of Sects—
31 Flavors of Religious Life

⊕ ⊕ ⊕ ⊕ ⊕ ⊕

Marozia

W hoever said that papal life had to be celibate? Or even law-abiding? Certainly not Marozia and her mother Theodora, a pair of pope makers and breakers whose well-documented careers could very well be the source of the persistent female pope stories of medieval times.

Tenth-century Rome, where Marozia got her smart start as the titled daughter of an important senator named Crescentii, was headquarters for all things papal; Vatican City hadn't been dreamed up yet. Like her outrageous mom Theodora, Marozia had a yen for religious men. Her first carnal coup was becoming the teen mistress to forty-something Pope Sergius III. Their association resulted in a love child named Johnny. But the divine Ms. M. had other fish to fry, and soon wed a royal fellow named Alberic, who was obliging enough to make Sergius III pope once again (Sergie had gone AWOL, a bit distracted by becoming a biological father.)

Then, in the disheveled recordkeeping and hurly-burly of tenth-century Italian politics, a new pope called John X somehow crept in. (By a tiny coincidence, he happened to be mother Theodora's latest lover.) Although John also tried to make nice by giving Marozia titles like "Senator" and "Noble," she just didn't take to the man. Nevertheless, Marozia had a certain amount of class. She waited until her mom died in 928 A.D. before throwing Pope John X in the slammer, suffocating him for good measure. By this time the papal office and the craven creatures in it were being called "a laughable pornocracy" by everybody.

Marozia had still further plans for the papacy. For a few years, though, she relaxed with her son, only taking a break from motherhood to vote in a stopgap pope or two of her own, all of whom disappeared mysteriously after brief reigns. When illegitimate little Johnny turned seventeen, she got back to business, installing him as Pope John XI.

She hadn't reckoned on the heartbreak of sibling rivalry. Her other son, Alberic Junior, soon got terribly jealous of the fun Marozia seemed to be having with son Pope John, who officiated at her latest incestuous wedding and made it possible for the newlyweds to become king and queen of Italy. Just when Marozia thought she had family and papal politics handled, things came to a screeching halt. Alberic emulated mom's way with a power play, kicking out his brother the pope, setting up his own handpicked pope, and watching the king of Italy run like a bunny.

As Marozia was dragged off to prison by her son's thugs, there to rot for 50 years, she couldn't help but glow with "Atsa my bambino!" pride. (She was still in jail when her grandson Octavian foisted himself on the long-suffering Italians as Pope John XII in 955, a man whose crimes in office managed to lower the tone of the papacy even further before his demise *in flagrante delicto* at age 24. Given this sort of behavior, no wonder that religious leaders in medieval times often felt the church could get along very well without a Holy Father!)

Angela of Foligno

L ike other important religious figures of her day, thirteenth-century Italian mystic Angela of Foligno fasted constantly, had ecstatic visions, sported bloody stigmata, and sought greater oneness with God through self-inflicted suffering and caring for the sick. Catherine of Siena, for instance, drank the pus of her patients. Another saintly Catherine ate lice and caught a case of plague by kissing a plague victim.

Looking for spiritual oneupmanship, Angela and a fellow nun washed the sores of lepers and then drank the water. Once she got a leprous scab stuck in her throat, which she described as "sweet as communion."

Angela wasn't always this omnivorously fearless. Born near Assisi in 1250, she married a loving man and had several children. In her thirties, she got a religious call. But it wasn't until after she lost her family abruptly through illness that she sold her home and possessions, gave the money to the poor, began a whip-and-burn self-abuse program, and joined the order of St. Francis, where she dictated her story to her uncle and confessor, a friar named Arnaldo.

In it, she said, "In that time, by the will of God, my mother, who was a severe obstacle to me, died. Then my husband and all my children died within a brief period. Since I had taken the path of the religious life, and had begged God to be released from every worldly tie, their death was a great consolation for me."

Why on earth would a religious woman say the cruel things that Angela of Foligno did? The medieval mindset: Sometimes the normal life of marriage and children was looked on as a real hindrance to spiritual development. Angela, for instance, had enjoyed sex with her husband, and felt guilty about it later.

Female mystics didn't need earthly sex partners—they had a direct and intimate relationship with God which, due to its totality, had a strong erotic component to it. Interestingly, the feelings of ecstacy and the sensuous metaphors of religious experience had been described first by *male* mystics—but Angela and other female mystics emulated them.

During the six years she spent dictating her visions and feelings to her confessor, Angela had a tremendous sense of frustration. Her desire to meld completely with God made her want to die at times. At other moments, she indulged in marathon l screaming fits outside local churches. To her mind, anyway, food was a symbol of human corruption and physicality. It's claimed that this holy anorexic of Foligno chalked up twelve years with nary a nosh or nibble—possibly making her a Guinness record holder.

In her *Book of Divine Consolation,* Angela concentrated on the theme of love between herself and God. By this time, even her inexplicably devoted followers were getting poor tortured Angela down. Before her death in 1309, the saint in the making said she wanted to streak naked through Foligno with chunks of dead fish and rotting meat around her neck, viewing herself as "this worthless woman, full of malice and pretense . . . do not adore this idol any more, because in this idol lives the devil." This aggressive inspiration to healthy living was beatified by the pope in 1693.

> *"Sometimes I see the host as if I were seeing a neck or breast in nobility and beauty exceeding those of the sun, and seeming to come from within. In the face of this beauty I understand without a shadow of a doubt that I am seeing God."*
>
> —Angela of Foligno

Pope Joan & Pope Manfreda

Popehood for women—the impossible dream, you say? Between 855 and 1300, legend has it, several bold females went for the big miter. Joan, the first wanna-be, came from a German-English background, and got to pope city via Athens, where she'd gone with her lover to study. Her awesome knowledge of scriptures supposedly got her elected Pope John VIII in 854; after two years in office, Joan experienced a miracle. Unfortunately, it was the miracle of birth—and it happened while on procession along a busy Roman street. Promptly stoned to death, the pregnant pope made a great bad example for centuries. Various chroniclers in Joan's time vouched for her existence, but her historicity has been quarreled over ever since.

In the late 1200s, Manfreda of Milan was touted as the first in a new series of feminine popes. Although Pope Manfreda had a good run, she and her followers were persecuted to the max. In 1300, this not-even pregnant spiritual leader was sent to the stake in Lombardy.

The post-pope trauma caused by these impertinent females brought about a new open-air policy: now papal candidates had to sit naked above a hole in the floor; from the view room below, the selection committee would holler joyfully, "He has testicles, and they hang just fine." (It sounds a bit more dignified in Latin.)

Clare of Assisi

Ever hear about television's own patron saint—Clare of Assisi? (Why the TV industry deserves holy protection, much less a saint, is unknown.) Like her childhood friend Francis, Clare was a rich kid, born (even before the advent of *radio*) in 1194. As a youngster, Clare admired Francis, whose way with animals and humans put him on the saintly fast track. In a world of pious frauds and holier-than-thou popes, Francis talked the talk and walked the walk; at eighteen, Clare followed suit, had her head shaved, and got busy begging for grits in her sackcloth. After founding the Poor Clares, an order whose actual poverty was a radical departure for nunneries of the day, Clare also helped establish the Franciscan Third Order, a nonconvent way of religious service open to women and men as civilians rather than nuns or monks. Before her death at sixty, she clairvoyantly "saw" a Christmas Mass across town—and that is how the most down-to-earth of saints came to be the icon for the most unreal medium of expression.

Reception's great—but where's Baywatch?

Hilda of Whitby

The most famous and energetic of English religious educators, Hilda spent thirty-two years teaching and establishing a network of monasteries and abbeys across England. Less known, and just as astonishing, her first three decades were spent as that Middle Ages rare bird, a single woman. An Anglo-Saxon princess from a landed family, young Hilda wasn't about to take any early vows—marital or monastic.

During her lifetime (614–80), Christianity came from Ireland and spread into Anglo-Saxon England. In her teens, Hilda became a Celtic Christian; with it she got the independence and visibility which Celtic women traditionally had—both in the church and as civilians. In her mid-thirties, Hilda finally made a career choice: she entered monastic life.

Just giving away all her things took awhile. She spent time with her sister Hereswith, a nun whose monastery was near Paris. But then the Bishop of Aidan gave Hilda a piece of English real estate, where she established a small monastery. Soon after, she was appointed to run an established religious house at Tadcaster.

These tenures clearly showed Hilda what talents she had as teacher and administrator. Other people saw them as well. King Owsia, who'd made a vow to give his daughter to a convent if he won a certain battle, liked Hilda's style; he gave her a big chunk of land, on which she founded Whitby monastery in 657. (Everything in life has strings attached, as Hilda found: She was obliged to take Owsia's daughter with the package—who turned out to be barely one year old. Religious daycare was off and running.)

In her double monastery, based on the Irish model, separate-but-equal communities of men and women sedulously followed Abbess Hilda's example of peace, charity, purity, and justice. A center of scholarship, Whitby grew rich in intellectual talent—a commodity which benefited the community as much as its tangible assets, also held communally. Five noted bishops trained at Whitby; Hilda herself may also have been ordained a bishop according to Celtic tradition. As chief educator, she taught theology, grammar, music, the arts, and medicine.

Larger monasteries like Whitby typically owned entire villages, forests, farming lands, and other churches. Besides her religious chores, Hilda administered local justice and did very secular tasks like collecting taxes.

She also discovered new talent. At the Whitby dinner table, humbler folk also ate and took part in the usual after-dinner entertainment—passing the harp and singing a song. Hilda noticed that Caedmon the cowherd had performance anxiety, and would always slip away. One night, he dreamt a man told him to sing about the creation, helpfully supplying a verse to use. The dream reached Hilda's ears—who took him away from bovine punching, got him into a literacy course, and gave him *carte blanche* to write verse. Not only did he delight Whitby's table, but Caedmon became famed as England's first vernacular Christian poet.

In 664, Hilda took a key role in the direction Christianity would take by hosting the Synod of Whitby. Although she favored the Celtic brand, the Synod voted to follow Roman forms of the church. Independent as she was, Hilda must have had a hard time acquiescing.

Hilda (called Mother by everyone) was greatly loved. When Hilda was a baby, her father was banished; her mother had a dream about searching for him but in vain. Then she spotted a jewel hidden under her clothes which scintillated with a splendor that seemed to light all of England. Hilda turned out to be that jewel.

Ende of Gerona

Taking advantage of the great interest in gloom, doom, and matters millenial, around 970 a Spanish painter named Ende created a highly imaginative series on the Apocalypse in book form. In Ende's day, the Catholic church was the only game in town so far as the production and illustration (called illumination) of sacred texts. We know little about the artist, other than that she was a nun and a woman of the upper classes. Ende had a very Spanish talent; the flowing lines, playful stars, semicomic dragons, and bands of color in her work transcend time to produce an effect more Joan Miró than Middle Age. A woman who gave credit where credit was due, she signed her work "Ende painter and (with) the help of God and Brother Emeterius Presbyter." The monk who served as her assistant has a style identified from another signed manuscript; scholars are confident that most of the Gerona Apocalypse illuminations are the work of Ende—and her supreme inspiration. Ende's artful manuscript can still be admired at the cathedral in Gerona, Spain, where she painted it.

Katherine Zell

One of many female activists for the early Protestant church, hard-charging Katherine had a blunt way with words. A native of Strasbourg (then Germany, now France), she embraced Lutheranism with the fervor of a Grateful Dead fan. Looking for even more involvement, she married an ex-priest turned Lutheran; the pair became leading reformers, keeping authorities on the boil.

Even after Katherine became the widow Zell, she lobbied Lutherans and Catholics alike for greater tolerance of religion, worked for better health facilities, and cared for the sick. After inspecting the local hospital, undiplomatic Zell huffed: "Besides food even the healthy wouldn't eat, the place is so Godless that when an 'Our Father' is said at the table, it's done so quietly that no one knows if it's a prayer or a fart. . . . The patients sleep in horrible beds, like a sow in her own manure." (Medieval patients usually slept two to a bed.) Her recommendations? "Appoint God-fearing women who will oversee things properly." Sadly, the proposals of this fearless Frau seldom got acted on—but her words give us a vivid picture of her times.

> *"A disturber of the peace, am I? Yes indeed, of my own peace. Do you call this disturbing the peace?.. instead of spending my time in frivolous amusements, I have visited the plague-infested and carried out the dead..."*

> —Zell's 1557 letter to the city of Strasbourg

Hildegard of Bingen

After a mock funeral ceremony, her parents said a final *"Auf Wiedersehen"* and locked eight-year-old Hildegard into a cell with the dimensions and comforts of a walk-in freezer. Was she a plague victim? Hopelessly insane? A budding young criminal of the Middle Ages? Believe it or not, incarceration as an anchorite or anchoress was chosen by many children and/or their parents. By 1098, when Hildegard was born in the Rhine district of Germany, there were countless kids in religious lockup. Unlike nuns, anchorites were required to stay in their cells until death.

A frail youngster, Hildegard had religious visions; her aristocratic parents decided to tithe her to God, placing her in a one-room, one-windowed enclosure at the Disibodenburg monastic order. This meager space was already occupied by Jutta, an anchoress lifer who taught the girl reading, writing, Latin, and music. Other than trips to the privy, Hildegard spent the next seven years in the lockbox.

By degrees, word spread about the child's extraordinary spiritual and intellectual gifts; other women who wished to study with her jammed into the space, which eventually turned her semisolitary confinement into—a nunnery. Sensing the contradiction, the powers that be commuted her solitary confinement into nun status (which also gave Hildegard a chance to see the rest of the monastery).

In her serene surroundings, Hildegard had ample time to develop the talents God had bestowed. More than two hundred years before the Renaissance was dreamed of, this woman displayed prodigious abilities as religious mystic, writer, composer, playright, healer, botanist, and administrator.

After Jutta died, Hildegard was elected to head up the fledgling group of nuns.

Her experiences running the convent—and later moving to new quarters and establishing a second convent on the Rhine—gradually turned her from a highly diffident person into a more self-assured woman.

When Hildegard turned forty-two, she had a vision that was decisive in her transformation from contemplative to activist. About it, she said, "A blinding light of exceptional brilliance flowed through my entire brain. And so it kindled my whole heart and breast like a flame, not burning but warming . . . and suddenly I was able to taste of the understanding of books. . . ." (Her visions are now thought to have been triggered by migraine; what sets her apart from other migraine sufferers is what she accomplished as a result of her illness.)

The writings from her unfettered mind included mystery plays, an opera, poems, and books. Their subject matter ranged from theology to natural history to healing. Among Hildegard's herbal tips: mandrake root would ease depression and love-sickness; camphor was useful for keeping nuns alert during Mass. She described 485 herbs and plants, among them, hops—the first written reference to them in beer-making.

For a sheltered virgin, Hildegard had some pretty frank things to say about sex—including what may be the first written description of the female orgasm. In our century, her musical legacy is getting equal attention from New Age and early music fans.

Female mystics were a dime a dozen in medieval times. Hildegard's prophetic message to the world, however, centered around the goodness of creation and God's pleasure in it. Naturally this upset the fire-and-brimstoners. To the end of her very long life, Hildegard fought for a tolerant, just, and positive spirituality in a European world echoing with an often hateful and narrow Christianity.

Adele Ehinger

By Adele Ehinger's day in fifteenth-century Germany, piety had taken a real nosedive. Once thought of as cloistered and chaste refuges from the world, some convents and nunneries had become downright riotous. That was the case in Ulm, where the wealthy patron of the convent got a little worried about the lack of cleanliness and godliness on-site, to say nothing of the hang-loose attitude.

A snoopy sort, he made a search of the premises and his worst fears were realized. Among other things, he found a batch of love letters received by Adele and the other nuns from their supposedly spiritual counterparts.

One steamy note to the scarlet "A" from a discreet, initials-only admirer read, "In truth I know of nothing on earth more charming than you alone and I suffer much secret pain in my heart when I cannot have you, my love, as my heart desires. . . . Think of me in the morning, and then I shall, God willing, be with you and talk to you about various things about which I really cannot write. I would have come on Sunday but the dress for us was not ready.".

The responses of the naughty nuns didn't turn up. However, their dismayed patron did discover that most were pregnant. Even after he spilled the beans to the women's relatives and issued a "Get thee *out* of the nunnery!" order, Adele and friends were in no great hurry to leave—and their interesting condition didn't give their relatives many gray hairs, either.

The disheveled and wayward life at the Ulm convent was par for the course, evidently—a corrupt climate which set the stage for the likes of reformer Martin Luther and Protestantism.

Maria Victoria della Verde

Goodness knows, you could never do too much praying, rosary-counting, and genuflecting in a sixteenth-century Italian nunnery. Nevertheless, a nun by the name of Maria Victoria della Verde found time on her hands. What to do? Maria and her advisors being Italian, the answer was: cook. Maybe even throw together a publication of, say, nice recipes from the nunnery. In the late 1500s, Maria embarked on her culinary quest. No wimpy little ecclesiastical foods in this collection: Besides pasta, pasta, pasta, she included that old favorite among women in religious orders, *strozzapretti*. A recipe for caloric, cholesterolic dumplings, strozzapretti translates as "priest stranglers." An in-joke among nuns—or wishful thinking from the distaff religious population? Maria left no answer to this, one of history's minor mysteries.

Radegund

Executive headhunters would have been all over Radegund—what a woman, what a leader, what an administrator! Granted, she had made a far from satisfactory queen of early France, according to her husband Lothar (also known as Lothar the loathsome). Of course, maybe that was her intent; if she'd been good at queening, Lothar wouldn't have let her become a nun. Clever Radegund!

Even as a child, Rad's life had been eventful. Snatched from her own Burgundian people as a child, this princess was put on hold in a convent until she became old enough to become queen of Lothar, her Frankish captor. She got a great education in the convent—especially considering this was sixth-century France. She also liked to play martyr (mortifying the flesh, pretending to be tortured) as any saint worth her hair shirt had been.

R's real martyrdom began the day she left the nunnery to marry Lothar. His violence toward her and her brother, coupled with Radegund's childlessness, led her to seek the sanctuary of religious life. She went on to found the famous monastery of Saint Croix at Poitiers, a center of learning that housed over 200 nuns, with amenities that included access to their own library (as rare as Camembert in that day and age).

Interested in medicine and healing as well as piety, abbess Radegund sold her jewels (one useful leftover from her rotten marriage) to build a hospital; eventually, many of her nuns at Poitiers studied healing methods. The abbess favored a therapy unusual for her times: she plunged patients into a bath, clambered in, then scrubbed them from head to foot with soap. Then she fed them a three-course meal. What a radical notion!

As abbess of her own nunnery, Radegund herself now got to play martyr to her heart's content—sleeping on ashes, wearing a veritable wardrobe of hair shirts, hauling firewood, and fighting to do KP duty. When not otherwise occupied, Radegund tossed off the occasional pious poem, sometimes engaging in poetic intercourse with the likes of famed Italian bard-in-residence Fortunatus—a secular activity that seemed a bit too racy for other abbesses, who dropped her a sniffy note to that effect. (After her death, Fortunatus would write a superpious *Saint's Life of Radegund*.)

Even the most saintly soul can exert only so much moral moxie, however—especially postmortem. Once Radegund died, the nuns at Poitiers took to quarreling in a most unseemly manner about the next head abbess. One of the sore losers led an armed attack on the winner and the monastery, killing a few of her sister nuns, and kidnapping the abbess-elect, requiring the nearby lord of the manor to intervene, SWAT-style. Even after the abbess was snatched back, the sore loser pressed her case, throwing accusations of sorcery, murder, and adultery about with abandon until a court order for her banishment finally came through. Radegund may have been a gentle and pious soul, but few people—nuns included—fit that description in the aggressive early days of proto-France.

Rabi'a al-Adawiya

icknamed "that woman on fire with love," Rabi'a al-Adawiya was not, as you might first think, a courtesan or a much-wed Baghdad starlet. Rather, she was a pivotal figure in the early development of Sufism, which is to Islam what mysticism is to Christianity. An ethical sect that renounced worldly comforts and embraced blissful union with a supreme being, Sufism also used music and dance as a path to spiritual ecstacy.

Born in 717, about a century after Mohammed the Prophet's death, Rabi'a sprang from a humble family, rich only in daughters. When they got to her, the parents had pretty much run out of naming ideas, so they called her "Rabi'a," meaning the fourth. Their poverty was tough enough. But then a terrible famine hit the city of Basra, the family got separated, and Rabi'a ended up alone, on the streets. Before long, a man who made a living from orphans' misfortunes sold her as a household slave for six dirhams.

Despite her hard life, Rabi'a had a strong contemplative bent. When her work was finished, she would stand in prayer until dawn. One night, her owner caught her contemplating so hard that a shining lamp appeared to be levitating over her head. Thoroughly spooked, he freed her immediately.

Rabi'a left her Persian Gulf port city of Basra and headed for a hermitage in the desert, where she could become a religious recluse and pursue celibacy and enlightenment in peace and quiet. Although unlettered, Rabi'a was a teacher and scholar, as famous for her Sufi sayings in prose and poetry as for her exemplary life. Naturally, once the word got around, the mystic started attracting fans, followers, and suitors. Hoping for a spirituality shortcut, rich new friends offered her money. When others pushed her to take it, she said, "I'd truly be ashamed to ask for worldly things from Him to whom the world belongs; so why would I ask for the same things from those to whom it does not belong?"

At another point in her life, Rabi'a set out to make her pilgrimage to the Islamic holy city of Mecca, nearly a thousand miles south and west of her simple quarters in the Iraqi desert. After loading up her donkey for the trip, she got on board. In mid-desert, however, the animal up and died; Rabi'a, alone and stumped, began to pray to God for help. Her powers of prayer were such, it was said, that the donkey came back to life—whereupon the holy woman jumped on and continued her pilgrimage.

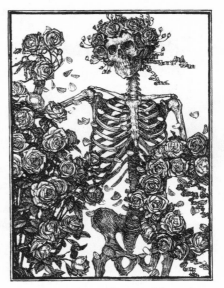

Sufism: now it's the Grateful Dead, a jug of wine, and thou

Unlike her Moslem contemporaries, she wasn't obsessed with heaven and hell either. Rabi'a's commitment to Divine Love, her simple and loving doctrine, made her one of Sufi's earliest high authorities. She lived to be eighty, a grand old woman later credited with many miraculous feats, from communicating with animals to making prayer rugs fly. Even without the miracles, her life bears witness to the spiritual stature even the humblest women sometimes attained. Poet and Sufi mystic Omar Khayyam may have gotten more famous, but Rabi'a reached a level of dignity and respect as holy as that given to any of the male mystics of Islam.

Lady Nijo & Murasaki

L ife was rugged in medieval Japan for women like Lady Nijo and Lady Murasaki. There was the daily grind of sake parties. The relentless ritual of selecting the absolutely right seven-layer silk gown to match the day and season from one's huge wardrobe. And the nonstop chores of writing a hand-calligraphed poem for every occasion, from the most fleeting of meetings to the most minor thank-you. These exquisite activities (and others not nearly so exquisite) absorbed Japan's aristocrats for centuries.

We think *we* live in a nostalgia-crazy society—Lady Nijo (born in 1257) and her sensitive pals based their entire lives on the actions, words, and behavior from a novel written in 1008 by another Japanese high-society woman!

Known only by the name of her heroine, Lady Murasaki, the author called her fifty-four-volume masterpiece *The Tale of Genji*. Although heavily fictionalized, *Genji* was based on Murasaki's own years of service to the Empress Akiko, to whom she taught Chinese literature on the sly. The mystery author also kept a diary of court life, its raw material eventually becoming her novel of Prince Genji and his loves. With this feat, this unknown Japanese genius created the world's earliest novel. A talented and bilingual artist, she also wrote poetry in Japanese and Chinese.

Two centuries after Murasaki, a small fourteen year old was given as a bed-toy to a Japanese emperor with the provocative name of GoFukasaka. The unwilling young concubine eventually became a compliant courtesan named Lady Nijo (Lady Second Avenue)—and an observer of court life whose acuity of vision and wit were the equal of earlier writer Murasaki.

In between love affairs and a child or two, Nijo also started a diary. After twelve years at court, this fun-loving social climber was expelled over some extra-curricular activity with old GoFukasaka's brother and political rival. Still a woman of great personal charm and talents in music, poetry, and painting, Lady Nijo shaved her head, gave up (with a wince perhaps) those gorgeous silk garments, and became a Buddhist nun.

In many respects, her book, a delicately acid and funny tell-all called *The Confessions of Lady Nijo*, echoes Lady Murasaki's masterpiece. Like one of those marvelous Oriental nested boxes, her story contains both her own poetry and echoes of the Heian culture of Murasaki which Nijo and her friends strove so hard to emulate.

There was one important difference between these two giants of Japanese literature, however: Nijo's book was nonfiction. In describing court capers, she used the real names of the all-too-human emperor and his family. That's why the book remained underground for more than six centuries. In 1940, a scholar stumbled across the only existing copy, disguised as a treatise on geography. Besides their value as history and literature, the works of geisha-turned-nuns Ladies Nijo and Murasaki reveal a universality of female experience that is startlingly contemporary.

Hroswitha

Besides having a name that was a mouthful, even for an Anglo-Saxon, Hroswitha gained a secure place on the "top forty nuns we'd like to immortalize" list of tenth-century Europe. Of noble birth, she wheedled an excellent education for herself, despite the Dark Ages disinterest in educating women.

Naturally Hroswitha had to enter a nunnery to do much of anything with her learning—or her knack for leadership. At age 23, she signed up for the Benedictine Abbey in Gandersheim, Germany.

Besides being superb at matters spiritual, Hroswitha had a tremendous and prolific talent for poetry, prose, drama, and math. In her book called *Sapientia*, for instance, she included fiendish problems that only true math nerds would relish—or be able to solve. For instance, the book's main character is asked how old her daughters Faith, Hope, and Charity are; instead of whipping out pictures, she answers that Faith is an oddly even redundant number, Hope is a defective evenly odd number, and Charity is a defectively evenly even number. (Worse yet, Hroswitha didn't provide a cheat-sheet for her conundrum—and don't look at *me* for help.)

Along with math and literary talent, Hroswitha harbored the shocking belief that piety went down better when leavened with humor. Besides composing drama and legends, she wrote six plays patterned after the classical Roman comedies of Terence. In a typical scene, three young virgins who are being attacked by a vicious Roman general call on God to avoid rape. God answers their prayers by making the general hallucinate; soon he's salivating over the pots and pans in the kitchen, caressing the kettles and getting unrecognizably black-faced with soot, while the girls giggle.

In 947, the abbey of Gandersheim became, through royal edict, what amounted to its own small country. The abbey had powers to mint coinage, hold court, answer directly to the pope without dealing with those sniffy bishops, and even field an army.

It's now thought that Hroswitha was a canoness, the most privileged type of religious resident, rather than a nun. As canoness, she would have the right to own land, keep her own set of servants, entertain guests, and move freely in and out of the abbey. (Highly uppity canoness types even left to get married if they pleased, with nary a Hail Mary or other pesky penance to be done.)

Although highly thought of during her life, Hroswitha wasn't thought of much at all for centuries after her death. Later generations, however, picked up on her creative work—an opus that

Medieval book signings: pope gets curtsey, first edition

stands up to the passage of time. Hroswitha herself had no grandiose illusions. After listening to bishops fret about her creations, this rollicking soul smiled and said, "If you do not much like them, at least they have pleased myself."

A Lust for Wander—Gotta Get Outta This Zip Code

Aud the Deep-Minded

A ud the Deep-Minded was a new breed of Viking—a kinder, gentler Norsewoman. After centuries of pillaging, piracy, and property snatching, her brand of behavior was more than welcome.

Born in 855, Aud grew up in the Scottish islands of the Hebrides, getting her spiritual depth from her mother, a Celtic Christian, and her direction-finding ability from dad Ketil Flatnose, a Norwegian Viking. After a brief spin at matrimony to a Dublin king named Olaf the White, the new divorcee and her son, Thorstein the Red, enjoyed several decades of peacefully micromanaging the Hebrides. Aud was busy spoiling her grandchildren and doing a little contemplation when along came a couple of Scots who hadn't gotten the word that mayhem was officially over, and killed Aud's son.

Opting to flee rather than fight, Aud built a ship, loaded it with big denomination currency, jammed her grandchildren and a band of followers on board, and hauled keel outta there. First she island-hopped to the Orkneys, where she married off a granddaughter to the local honcho; then to the Faroes, where she did ditto. While scenic, both places seemed way too cramped for a gal who was used to something more in the 2,900-square-mile range.

Aud's two brothers were already in a place with the unpromising name of Iceland. When the Deep-Minded One heard the details, however, she shooed everyone back in the ship and set off. Some three hundred horribly seasick miles across the north Atlantic Ocean, Aud and company spotted an ample chunk of land. Before she could even announce, "We're here!" the ship hit a reef and sank, giving everyone a chance to see just how cool Iceland's waters were. (Thankfully, most on board had swimming or timber-clinging skills.)

On shore, a bedraggled Aud counted heads. The grandkids made it; ditto some twenty faithful followers, a number of slaves, and most of grandma's treasures, now a soggy mass of flotsam and jetsam.

You thought that shipwreck was a cold experience—you should have seen the welcome Aud's brother Helgi gave them. One look, and he said, "Only room for ten of the least squishy." Aud steamed off to her other brother's, who was wise enough not to push his luck with the kinder, gentler Viking thing.

Once dry, our senior explorer borrowed a boat and began circling Iceland, examining the deeply indented coast, and setting a bonfire wherever she saw some property she fancied to officially stake her claim. At the end of her shopping trip, Aud had claimed about 180 square miles.

Now it was divvying up time—and grandma had a ball. Followers, grandkids, and slaves got huge parcels, marked with Christian crosses. One granddaughter got an entire river valley as a dowry; Aud sprang for the wedding besides. As her final official act, Grandma Deep choreographed the marriage of her youngest grandson. At the reception, she greeted the guests, made sure the ale was flowing—and then went off to her eternal rest. At her request, this best and brightest of the Viking matriarchs was buried on Iceland's coast, in the salty land below the high-water mark.

Inés de Suárez

Husbands: they're nothing but headaches, thought thirty-something Inés de Suárez, when hers failed to come home from conquistadoring in South America. She needed a little outing, anyway—time to go look for him.

In 1537, Inés sailed from Spain to the New World, only to find after tramping from Venezuela to Peru that Señor Suárez had died in the siege of Cuzco. While pondering what to do, the new widow kept busy as a nurse—a skill that proved handy when she joined the expedition of conquistador Pedro de Valdivia, setting out to discover whatever. (As it turns out, a compass might have been useful, too.)

Looking for a likely place to establish a capital in Chile, Pedro managed to get them lost in the driest place on earth—the Atacama Desert. Inés, however, managed to save the expedition by discovering a fresh-water spring. (By now, she was both nurse and straw boss for nearly a thousand Indians who were carrying the supplies.)

In February of 1539, Pedro finally found a piece of terrain that struck him as capital material. On the spot, he called it Santiago, and Inés set about making it her new home. You know these itchy-footed conquistadores, though—by September, he was off again to subdue rebels in the south.

In Pedro's absence, thousands of Indians attacked Santiago. Despite being outnumbered, Inés and the remaining Spaniards captured the seven rebel chiefs. Displaying a real gift for tactics, Inés voted to behead the chiefs, decapitated the first one herself, and tossed the bloody trophy at the attackers, who were demoralized enough so that the Spaniards could mop them up with a cavalry charge.

A few days later, Pedro showed up, to find most of Santiago burned down. However, our valiant female city-founder was able to save a few trinkets, some wheat, and a couple of animals from the flames. By the time a supply ship from Spain arrived in 1543, Inés had gotten the city's pig and chicken population to procreate into the thousands, and her green thumb had bread on every table.

Although the widow Suárez and Pedro had a romance going for years, he never did pop the question—a small but sticky matter of a wife still back in Spain. Finally fed up, the energetic Inés married Rodrigo de Quiroga, one of Pedro's lieutenants. The following year, the conquistador retirement fund awarded her land and money to build the church of our Lady de Monserrat on Santiago's hill of Cerro Blanco.

When she was 46, Inés no doubt got a certain wry amusement out of a new arrival—Pedro Valdivia's wife from Spain. Mrs. Valdivia hurried off the boat, only to find that she was a widow. Not only had her hubby Pedro been killed in a recent battle with the local Indians, he had thoughtfully left her 200,000 pesos—of debts. (Where's that aspirin, Inés?)

Catalina de Erauso

L ife sentence as a nun in a convent? Fate worse than death, thought Basque spitfire Catalina de Erauso, upon reaching those troubled teenage years. Stuffed into a nunnery by her folks, Catalina ran away in March of 1600. Her goal: to join the opposite sex. Unlike other women who put on male duds and told the barber "short all around," Catalina wasn't chasing a sweetheart, husband, or a prized client—this tall, well-muscled tomboy craved an adventurous life. And she got it. A natural at cross-dressing, swordplay, and skullduggery, Catalina freelanced across Spain; three years later, she earned (or stole) her passage to the New World. Once she started rambling across Panama, Peru, and Chile, Erauso really came into her own as a brawler, gambler, and soldier of fortune.

Occasionally she held a legitimate job. She joined the army, became a second lieutenant, and served under her older bro Michael, fighting the Indians. But Catalina had a hair-trigger temper and a real talent with pistols, daggers, and swords. Not counting battlefield slayings, she murdered eight men, only one of whom she was sorry about—the "mistaken identity" killing of her own sibling in a nighttime duel.

For 20-odd (very odd) years, gender-bender Erauso roamed the Wild West highlands of the Peruvian Andes, in and out of jail, evading the law (and twice the hangman's noose) by a hair. Like other Dirty Harrys, she attracted female admirers but evaded the snare of intimacy—or matrimony.

In 1620, finding herself in a worse jam than usual, Catalina sought refuge with a bishop—and then confessed her true story. Despite her seamy life, Erauso was still a virgin; this astounded the bishop more than anything. In fact, people seemed to feel this marvel compensated for her prior sins! She returned to Spain a celebrity; a gifted talker, she schmoozed the king into awarding her a pension and a return ticket, then visited the pope, who was tickled enough to give Catalina, now widely known as "the Lieutenant Nun," the all-clear to wear male clothing. When last heard of, Catalina was mule-driving in Mexico, calling herself Antonio de Erauso.

Even before her death, legends built around the Lieutenant Nun. Probably penniless when she died, this scalawag left something priceless—an autobiography of her capers. It gives a glimpse of a bold and original mind—and the high price she paid for the lone gun, "don't tie me down" life.

Marie Guyart

Even the most cynical heart has to pity the postal carrier who worked Marie Guyart's route in a rural corner of seventeenth century French Canada. She's estimated to have sent more than 33,000 letters! When supernun Marie wasn't founding convents, heading the Ursuline Order in Canada, and leading missionary expeditions to Indian tribes, she was writing letters home to France. Marie's own Priority Mail message from God came in 1631, after which she entered a convent and began creating mystical writings. Eight years later, she and three other adventurous women emigrated to the New World, leaving her son with her sister, and the flood of transatlantic mail began. Over 200 of her chatty notes still exist, giving a marvelous Marie's-eye view of early Canada.

Kenau Hasselaar

A Dutch brewer's daughter in sixteenth-century Haarlem, Kenau didn't just say "Ya, ya" to the first set of clog shoes who pulled up and honked. She married a hometown shipwright, who built new ships and repaired old ones while she happily built a home life until widowed at thirty-five, with four kids to support. Fortunately, hometown Haarlem was a happening port and trade center, strategically located a tulip bulb's throw from Amsterdam.

In 1562, widow Haselaar registered with city authorities as an independent shipwright and jumped into the high-mileage life of medieval business folk. You had to be hard as Gouda cheese rind to make it as an entrepreneur. (In fact, Dutch female traders became famous in the Old World and the New as very tough cookies in Kenau's time and the next century.)

Kenau put in long days, working the Holland-Belgium-Sweden-Denmark circuit. Besides going after new ship orders and customers, she had to contend with tax-happy officials, lawsuit-happy colleagues, integrity-challenged suppliers, a recalci-trant workforce, and slick financiers—a business world quite like today, in fact. With her native wit and growing business acumen, Kenau soon became a person of standing even among the tough-to-impress Dutch.

But her feats as head of Hasselaar shipwright enterprises paled beside her actions as a loyal citizen. From a predominantly Protestant city, around 1568 Kenau and all the rest of Haarlem exploded in protest at the Catholic rule being imposed by Spanish Duke of Alba and his crowd. Hostilities broke out; along with other women, Kenau and her sister Amaron grabbed swords and jumped to the city's defense. Always good at management, Kenau organized a battalion of 300 female patriots, and led the charge herself. Although the Dutch kept the Spaniards from taking Haarlem, troops surrounded the city. After a dreadful seven-month siege, the starving locals surrendered, followed by the kind of deplorable aftermath you can read about in any newspaper today.

Five years later, however, Haarlemers won their city back. And Kenau received special kudos for her take-charge actions in the city's defense—an honor this Dutch treat relished until her death at over sixty.

Spaniards take Haarlem—Kenau and survivors take it back

Marguerite de la Roque

arguerite de la Roque really put the *wild* in wilderness. At first, it was kind of fun, being the first white woman to confront the vast expanses of North America. Gradually, however, it dawned on her: In the umpteen square kilometers of this brand-new territory called French Canada, she had *no one* to go shopping with.

Marguerite's story began in France, when she learned in 1541 that her cousin, a stuffed shirt named Roberval, was about to sail to the New World on another expedition with his explorer-partner, Jacques Cartier. Miss Marguerite heard the name *Cartier* and thought jewelry—an easy mistake to make. (Cartier did have a habit of flashing ersatz gold and diamonds—pieces of pyrite and quartz, actually—at passengers to encourage colonists for Canada.) Marguerite wheedled her way onto the ship, thinking, "transatlantic cruise—what a blast! Oh, and *garçon*, make that a double stateroom—I need to take my maid Damienne, of course."

The sea voyage was every bit as exciting as the madcap madamoiselle had anticipated—maybe even more so. The trip took months, ample time for the results of Marguerite's *ooh-la-la* with a male passenger to become ripely obvious. At this point, Robby finally tore himself away from Jacques and the riches they were going to discover and took note of his cousin's interesting condition. Feeling somewhat *bleu*, Roberval postponed a family feud until the ship was well up the Saint Lawrence River.

With a French flourish, he gave a "last stop for certain poorly behaved passengers—*au revoir, ma cherie!*" speech and unceremoniously dumped his cousin and her maid onto the sands of a small island. Family honor once more intact, he set sail.

Before Marguerite even had time to get lonely, her lover jumped ship and swam to the island thoughtfully laden with a few provisions, a pair of guns, and some ammo.

Despite her advancing pregnancy, Marguerite set about making the best of it, and soon had everyone building her a cabin. Tragically, her lover and maid weren't as resilient. Poor Madamoiselle M. had to babysit her boyfriend's corpse in the cabin all winter until she could bury it. Then she had to act as midwife at her own childbirth, which didn't go well, either. The baby soon died, making the population at the island cemetery jump to three—a darned sight bigger than the living population.

Alone with her memories, Canada's female Robinson Crusoe shot a bear from time to time, read her New Testament, and ate way too many berries. Two and a half years later, a fishing boat happened by. Despite being in utter rags, a highly persuasive Marguerite managed to hitch boat rides clear back to *la belle France*.

There, the gossipy grapevine soon spread the incredible details of her adventures as far as Spain, where they caught the imagination of another Marguerite, Queen of Navarra, who transmogrified the whole hard-breathing story into a saintly act of heroics in her book, the *Heptameron*. And Miss de la Roque, you ask? Not being able to find a position that utilized her hard-won skills in bear hunting and gravedigging, *la petite voyageuse* took up schoolmarming in Picardy.

María de Estrada

When Hernan Cortés and his band of Spanish roughnecks hit Mexico in 1519, introducing themselves and their Christian god as the act to follow, local Aztecs were shocked. Shortly thereafter, the Indians got another jolt when a white woman on horseback appeared in battle. Was this the Virgin Mary the foreigners kept talking about? Or had they consumed a bit too much peyote the night before, perhaps? As her dazzling swordwork soon showed, this *conquistadora*—although a vision—was no hallucination.

María de Estrada was the only Spanish woman—in fact, the only white woman of any nationality—in Mexico. From southern Spain, this ball of fire and her husband, Pedro Sánchez Farfán, had crossed the great pond together. Pedro must have been a standup guy. When María made it known she wanted to come to the New World in a fighting rather than a cheerleading capacity, Pedro obviously shrugged, "Why not?" Like other seasoned veterans with Cortés, the caballero couple from Sevilla had served in Hispaniola and probably Cuba before they joined the expedition to Mexico. (Incidentally, María and the other conquistadores had built-in motivation to do well. To join the expedition of Cortés, you had to invest in it first—no small sum, either.)

This venturesome woman didn't merely make cameo battle appearances. None of this "passing in review and rallying the troops with a heartwarming speech," as queens with wars to win were fond of doing. María, in full armor, jumped in feetfirst. Just like the men, she got eaten alive by local mosquitoes and ate rat with thistle sauce and other strange dishes.

At the horrendous battle inside Tenochtitlán, the capital city of Montezuma's Mexico, María distinguished herself, gaining the nickname "great lady" from the

Aztecs for her remarkably murderous way with a sword. She did equally well defending the bridge when the Spaniards fought their way out of the capital during what came to be called *noche triste* or "sad night." Later, at Otumba, she dazzled both sides with her lance capabilities from horseback.

After the fall of the Mexican capital, Commander Cortés threw a special banquet party, inviting only those who had fought well. María de Estrada made the guest list. She probably made the party, too—being a *sevillana*, she had nonstop dancing feet.

What an amazing all-nighter that must have been, on a shore thousands of miles from Spain—the men still in their quilted armor, flirting with María and a handful of other (noncombatant) women, all of them gorging on turkey and pork and wine brought from Vera Cruz, gambling and laughing, hooting and hollering and fandangoing up a storm, electric with the notion of their own Spanish Catholic God-ordained triumph.

Onorata Rodiana

"Renaissance woman" doesn't offer enough scope to describe Onorata Rodiana, a versatile native of Castelleone, Italy, whose talent for art was only surpassed by a bigger one for banditry. A fresco-painting whiz, Onorata was hired by the Marquis Gabrino Fondolo to decorate his palace in Cremona. While she was working on her painting commission, a lecher around the palace tried to fondolo our Onorata. She dropped her brushes, picked up a weapon (her palette knife?), stabbed the would-be rapist, and left the vicinity in a big hurry, disguised as a man.

The marquis—a real tyrant who would get his in 1425—pitched a fit, sending his troops after her but with zero results. After he cooled down, he put the word out on the street that Onorata could return any time, stabbing incident forgotten. Well, the marquis might find it easy to overlook the attack on Rodiana's person, but she was not about to buy into his "No harm, no foul" approach.

Anyway, she'd already found a new métier; by now, this marvelously flexible Ms. had plunged enthusiastically into a career field that offered more scope for her newfound skills. Rodiana joined a band of *condottieri*, the mercenaries for hire who made life in Renaissance Italy so exciting.

Never good at following orders, Onorata was soon giving them, as she climbed the corporate criminal ladder to eventually head up her own band. Over the next thirty years, the many-faceted Rodiana. found she could have it all: one week she was cross-dressing and masterminding the next plunder and pillage campaign; the next week, she would take on the occasional fresco odd job.

Although the art game had its peaks and valleys, banditry certainly didn't. Like modern attorneys, mercenaries throughout Italy knew the way to success in business was to keep on billing. Rodiana and her pay-per-pillage professionals got really good at milking would-be ruler clients, switching sides to milk clients' sworn enemies, prolonging small wars, and keeping regional hatreds alive—all done from horseback to minimize casualties. (*Condottieri* had their own code of ethics regarding bloodshed and major injuries, which resembled that of contemporary professional wrestling.)

The only thing our Renaissance rover forgot was: You can't go home again. In 1472, she returned to Castelleone, which was busy being beseiged by the Venetians. Always a softie for the hometown, Onorata tried to ride to the rescue, and was killed—nonstop action to the last frame.

Isabella d'Este

I t was a tough job, being the woman who invented dozens of perfumes and designer handcreams, kept a menagerie of monkeys and jesters on hand to amuse, and constantly jet-setted her art-loving farthingales around Europe—but hey, somebody had to do it. Are we talking about a total airhead of the Italian Renaissance? No way; Isabella d'Este had a political agenda behind her lavish wanderlust—and brains to match her extravagance.

This rosy-cheeked firstborn started out with certain advantages (like being the granddaughter of the king of Naples), which gave her as good a classical education as any boy-child. Rather than kicking back in class, dreaming about new dresses, Isabella cracked the books. Her idea of fun was map study and reading the classics in Latin and Greek.

Her bookwormish passion had a gratifying effect on Renaissance printing. Besides collecting first editions and luxury books written and illustrated by hand, imperious Isabella became a major patron (and sometimes the nightmare client) of high-end printers like Aldus Manutius of Venice. Occasionally she acted as publisher, commissioning the first print runs of the poetry of Petrarch and Virgil, and St. Jerome's *Letters*. She was one picky customer: in 1505, she wrote a snappish note to Aldus, returning four volumes and saying, "When you print some more, at a fair price and on finer paper, with more careful corrections, we shall be glad to see them." (At Isabella's request, Aldus also printed the very first book to be given page numbers, so we have that to thank her for.)

Snotty as Isabella could be, she did put out immense sums as an arts patron. She commissioned works from all the big names, from Raphael to Bellini. Her palaces were by Correggio and Michelangelo; her portraits by Titian, Rubens, and da Vinci.

Married at sixteen to the heir next door, a fellow more at home riding a warhorse than composing sonnets, she got to go her own headstrong way much of the time. In 1509, her husband the Marquis of Mantua was taken prisoner. Through her nonstop travels and house parties, Isabella had set up her own spy network, which let her to keep tabs on the political situation throughout Europe. Although her connections couldn't spring the marquis, Isabella and her unflinching way of taking command kept Mantua from being invaded. Her husband didn't appreciate these qualities; after wobbling out of prison in 1512, he said, "We're ashamed that it is our fate to have as wife a woman who is always ruled by her head."

Isabella retorted, "Your Excellency is indebted to me as never husband was to wife. Even if you loved and honored me more than anyone in the world, you could not repay my good faith." She then stalked off; their separation continued until his death, when Isabella set about running her son Freddie's life as the new marquis of Mantua.

Sadly, neither Isabella's marriage nor her kids fulfilled their original promise; in her long life of sixty years, her keen mind only got to oversee the doings of her own court, and for a time, to rule an Italian state of little importance. Despite her Renaissance abilities, Europe mainly thought of Isabella d'Este as its arbiter of art and fashion. In fact, the stylishly empty-headed ladies of the French court once wheedled their king to ask Isabella for a doll dressed like herself—so that all of them could dress in exactly the same manner.

Sophia Brahe

A determined Dane in an era when most rich girls played demure, Sophia Brahe wanted to travel far in life. As her Latin-spouting brother Tycho, already a celebrity astronomer at 17, said, "*Ad astra per aspera*—you can get to the stars, but it's a rocky road." She was willing to work; like her big brother, Sophia was crazy about anything celestial. But first there was the sticky matter of getting a scientific education. Unable to attend the males-only university, Sophie lobbied her well-fixed parents until she got home tutoring in math, music, astrology, alchemy, medicine, genealogy, and classical literature. As a bonus, Sophia studied observational astronomy with her brother, who was already getting one percent of the Danish government's annual budget for his research work on everything from comets to chemistry.

Both siblings had a stubborn side. Once Ty got into a duel with a student over math. Adrenalin pumping, they failed to notice it was a December night; Tycho lost most of his nose to a lucky stab in the dark, and thereafter had to wear a fake beak made of a gold-silver-copper alloy.

By her teens, Sophia had learned enough to become Tycho's assistant at Uraniborg, his lavishly funded observatory and scientific community on the island of Hven, where she helped with the computations for a lunar eclipse in 1573. Even sexier sky events were in store; the great comet of 1577, for instance, which blazed across the heavens when Sophia was 21. (Now *that* would have been a nice night for a duel.)

Eventually, Sophia had to drop her astronomical workload and marry a highborn gent of Skane, a part of southern Sweden annexed to Denmark at the time.

Already privileged by birth, Sophia became quite wealthy with her marriage. A mere decade later, her husband died. Sophia returned to her studies, tackling chemistry, biology, and horticulture this time.

She became a regular fixture at Uraniborg. Tycho had a high opinion of her work and needed her help, fixing the positions of 1,000 stars for his *magnum opus*. Sophia also mingled well with the science crowd, who stayed on the island for months at a time. One wonk she took a special shine to was Erik Lange, an upper-crust alchemist. She checked their astrological charts—a perfect match! Erik owned as much real estate as Sophia, so there was fiscal equilibrium as well as zodiac alignment. In 1590, they got engaged.

But soon this made-in-heaven merger began to crumble. Sophie's fiance ran up big debts, lost his holdings, and hightailed it for Germany. Thinking to cheer her up, Tycho wrote a poem in the form of a letter from Sophia to Erik, called *Urania Titani*, portraying a woman torn between hope and despair. The poem depressed Sophia even further—she couldn't read Latin, the only gap in her otherwise impeccable curriculum.

The hardheaded widow still believed she and Erik were fated to end up together. By now, not even Ty was on her side. After his death, and over the shouts of "You're disowned!" from the rest of the Brahe clan, Sophia left home to marry her alchemist in 1602. She now realized she had true love—but the stars had decreed her alchemy-obsessed hubby would never earn a living. After they ran through her fortune, Sophie put her expensive education to use by casting horoscopes and doing a little freelance doctoring—which kept her afloat even after Erik's death. A long and rocky road to travel: but Sophia probably read that in the stars, too.

Catherine de' Medici

atherine de' Medici was the Johnny Appleseed of her century; strategic alliances—also known as marriages—made by upperclass women like her often had more profound impact on their times than war or natural disaster. (Come to think of it, Catherine and her inept passion for political wheeling and dealing could qualify as a natural disaster also.)

When this wisp of a dishwater blonde with the soulful Italian eyes traveled to marry French King Henry II in 1533, she arrived with a fleet of twenty-seven ships for her entourage and belongings. Besides a dowry of five cities and a knockout array of oversized diamonds, rubies, and pearls, she carried innovations and ideas.

At first, the fourteen-year-old bride stuck to fun stuff. She issued a decree to the ladies in her court: "No waistlines bigger than thirteen inches!" (Before she began having ten babies, Medici wore a girdle with the signs of the zodiac worked in jewels to show off her tiny middle.)

Then she introduced some decent eats to the primitive Frenchies she'd married into—broccoli, haricot beans, and that surefire aphrodisiac, the artichoke. (Not that it seemed to work very well for *her*: during her 26-year marriage with Henry, he spent most of his ardor on Diane de Poitiers, his toothsome mistress.) Queen Catherine consoled herself by having her cooks whip up a few toothsome delights of her own, like macaroons, fruit sorbets, and truffles. (The French later claimed all of them as national dishes; ditto the double boiler, which Catherine had brought with her from Florence.)

Drawn by the glitter of her Medici name, a fellow named Machiavelli wrote a how-to book called *The Prince* for Catherine; unluckily for European politics, she read it, and after being widowed at forty, charged into action. Her misguided efforts to make backroom deals and religious compromises kept the Catholics and the Huguenots (French Protestants) constantly on the boil. To bring closure, she talked her green young son, King Charles, into ordering the Saint Bartholomew massacre (where 10,000 Protestants bit the dust) to tidy things up. It didn't.

Temporarily stumped by religious violence, Catherine turned to personal goals—like ruling Europe through her children and the marital alliances they made. To bring this off, it'd be handy to foresee the future, she thought. Catherine was superstitious as well as religious. Besides her faith in astrology and séances, she always wore a big honker of a talisman, its contents of blood and magical formulas supposed to give second sight. But she needed more firepower: who better than Nostradamus, the man whose uncanny predictions had foretold her hubby's death? The queen invited him for a midnight séance; gossip linked the two as lovers—so perhaps the séance included a side of artichokes.

Impressed by the visions he summoned up, Catherine was floored by his predictions of rotten reigns and short lives for her children. Her youngest, King Henry, was even more disastrous than Nostradamus had foreseen. A manic-depressive, gay Henry went from all-night party guy to religious flagellant—sometimes in the same week. Then he got crazy for lap poodles, whose fur resembled the Harpo look favored by the king and his fluffy male followers. Worst of all, Henry ignored his mom's advice—and his judgment calls were even worse than Catherine's.

The morose Queen Mother needed more than clairvoyance to salvage her game plan. It was enough to drive a Medici to drink—or a newer vice, perhaps. Luckily, Catherine had just the thing: Thanks to her international reputation and her interest in anything new, an ambassador had sent her the leaves of a substance guaranteed to calm and cheer—he called it tobacco.

Maysun

I guess Muawiya I, the first Arab caliph to govern North Africa and other pieces of Middle East real estate in 661, never heard of poetic license. But he soon learned about poetic justice, thanks to his wife Maysun, a comely Bedouin poet from the Syria desert. Once they had a son, the caliph installed Maysun and family in an amazing palace located in his shiny new capital of Damascus, which liked to think of itself as the city that invented conspicuous consumption. Far from the austere beauty of the desert, locked in an urban existence of shop-shop-shop, Maysun became desperately unhappy. The caliph didn't seem to catch her drift, either. Being a poet, she expressed herself in beautiful (and scimitar-sharp) words that have survived to our day:

> I love the Bedouin's tent, caressed by the murmuring breeze,
>> and standing amid boundless horizons
> More than the gilded halls of marble in all their royal splendor . . .
>> I prefer a desert cavalier, generous and poor,
>> to a fat lout in purple living behind closed doors.

Busy as he was with governing duties, her chubby hubby got tweaked in a major way at the "fat lout in purple" line and banished Maysun from the palace. Where did he send her? The worst place he could think of—the spot any Allah-fearing caliph on the way up would shun—the desert. Maysun probably chuckled all the way to the oasis.

Alvild

Being the Swedish princess of Gotland was no fun, Alvild thought. Besides zero sunbathing half the year, young Alvild was confined to quarters—and her father gave her a pair of poisonous snakes as pets to keep away pesky suitors. Finally, however, a gorgeous Dane named Alf showed up, ready to take the "kill the vipers and win the blonde" challenge. Despite Alf's snake-killing abilities, mom and dad disapproved of the liaison.

After listening to their relentless sermonizing, Alvild rustled up some outdoor gear and ran away, to pursue her own Dark Ages dream of becoming a pirate. A natural leader, Alvild headed for the nearest group of like-minded fitness and fortune-hunting females, becoming the top skull-and-crossbones of her own pirate band.

One day, while Alvild and her crew lurked in a Finnish harbor, who should show up but a wolfpack of Danish pirate vessels. Always a believer in "the best defense is a good offense," Alvild attacked straightaway. In the bloody battle that ensued, the Danes couldn't help noticing how *shapely* their opponents were. The lead rogue of the Danes jumped onto Alvild's ship, killing her crew right and left, trying to get to her. At that point, someone knocked off Alvild's helmet and she found herself at the wrong end of a cutlass held by none other than her old suitor, Alf. Trying to make the best of the fact that he'd killed various of her seafaring shipmates, Alvild melted when Alf claimed he'd been searching for her on land and sea. Evidently this swashbuckling Swede had had her fill of soloing on the bounding main. Soon she and Alf married and produced a treasure (legal, for once) of their own, a baby girl named Gurith.

Got a Brain,
Not Afraid to Use It

❖ ❖ ❖ ❖ ❖ ❖ ❖

Nzinga Mbande

Women conducting high-level negotiations in Africa during the 1600s? Child's play for Nzinga Mbande, the king's sister and official in charge of forging a lasting peace between the slave-rich land of Ndongo (known today as Angola) and Portugal, its slave-hungry colonizer. Naturally, the white guys tried a few psychological ploys, thinking they would rattle and/or humiliate this African arbitrator. Once, they brought Nzinga to where their governor was seated but neglected to put out a chair for her. Instead of protesting, she ordered one of her slaves to get on his hands and knees; sitting on the back of this human "chair," she wheeled and dealed all day. (Some accounts say that after the meeting, Nzinga toyed further with European minds by having Mr. Chair executed on the spot.)

When the official bickering was done, Nzinga liked nothing better than to kick back with a personal concubator or two. It was an article of faith among Ngolans—at least those with tons of status—that you can never have too many concubators. The male equivalent of the more familiar concubine or palace mistress, Nginza's harem of fifty-odd concubators answered to female names and dressed fit to kill in feminine finery.

Speaking of fit to kill: In 1624, Nzinga's brother was bumped off, and she became queen. After she filled her cabinet with women, the Portuguese broke the peace treaty. With a sigh of relish, Nzinga threw off her diplomatic posture and prepared her troops for war. Believing that females shouldn't hog just the cushy desk jobs, the queen called up women as well as men for the armed forces. To lead her warriors, she and her two fierce sisters, Kifunji and Mukumbu, wore matching animal-skin outfits and carried personal arsenals of sword, ax, and bow and arrows. By this time, Nzinga and family had also called it quits with the Christianity imported by the Portuguese and went back to good ole ritual cannibalism.

Although Kifunji was killed in battle, Nzinga and Mukumbu really got into the spirit of things, continuing to fight the Portuguese until the late 1650s. As you might expect, the prospect of being the object of ritual cannibalism had a negative effect on Portuguese morale. In addition, Nzinga had the bright idea of attacking and conquering other African kingdoms, which allowed her to build a confederacy (however involuntary) big enough to beat the enemy. She also formed alliances with the Dutch, intending to move against them once she'd gotten the other Europeans out of her hair.

In 1659, this spirited leader finally signed a treaty of peace and friendship with the Europeans she had fought for thirty-five years. An African queen to the last, Nzinga lived into her eighties—still bright-eyed and fond of noshing on human flesh now and then. All the attention lavished by those concubators must have done its job. Even today, Nzinga's nifty deeds are remembered, and the gorier ones glossed over, in the history books of Angolan schoolchildren. After Angola regained its independence in the twentieth century, grateful citizens named a boulevard in the capital after her.

Deborah Ascarelli

uring the late 1500s in Italy, making poetry was a lot more popular than making pasta. There were numerous educated and creative women in Renaissance Italy—and not merely Christian noblewomen, either. Deborah Ascarelli and many other literate Jewish women of the comfortable middle classes also seized opportunities to create and to be patrons of the arts. The wife of a successful merchant, Deb wrote poetry in Hebrew and Italian. Her skill with both languages also led her to translate hymns and several well-known books into Italian. Deborah's poetry made her famous in her country; her work came out in a 1601 edition—perhaps the first such example and one of the few to survive to our time. Three centuries later, in the pre-Mussolini era, one of her descendants republished her poetry—a poignant and pointed reminder to Fascists of the cultural contribution Italian Jews had made:

> *Although a beautiful shock of golden hair swings across*
> *her forehead*
> *And love finds nourishment in her eyes*
> *The chaste Susannah never strays from the right path*
> *And harbors not one thought without the Lord.*

Queen Sonduk

Even at age seven, a young Korean miss named Sonduk was a sharp observer and thinker. She happened to be around when her dad, the Korean king, received a gift package from China; in the box were some peony seeds, accompanied by paintings of the flower. Little Sonduk said, "Nice bloom—too bad it doesn't smell pretty!" Nonplussed, her dad asked why she said that. "If it did, there would be butterflies and bees around the flowers in the painting." Sure enough, when put to the test, the peonies came up scentless. Dad knew he had a brilliant daughter—and an excellent heir prospect. (He might not have been so hasty with praise had he known more about bees and butterflies, who are drawn by infrared designs on flowers as often as by the scent. On the other hand, he was grateful that Sonduk was sharp, given that he had no other heirs to continue the Silla dynasty.)

In her fourteen-year stint as queen of Korea, Sonduk used her wits and keen powers of observation to best advantage. The seventh century was a bloody, violent age for Korea; Sonduk had her hands full, keeping the country in equilibrium. (At least her domain remained in one piece.) As an educator, she activated the international exchange of intellectual ideas, often sending Korean scholars to China for that purpose. One of the legacies left by this keen-eyed woman is the Tower of the Moon and Stars, recognized as the first observatory in the Far East. Now a tourist draw, its tower still stands in Kyongju, South Korea, the capital city of long-ago Silla kings and queens like Sonduk.

Molly Frith

Her rap sheet was a mile long, her personal habits left a lot to be desired, and her aliases included "Moll Cutpurse" and the "Roaring Girle." Who was she? Just the most unrepentant female crook and cutup England ever had, that's who. The English love an all-arounder, and Molly Frith didn't disappoint. Born about 1589, Frith got her first nickname from her talent at robbing pedestrians by cutting their purse strings. It soon became evident to admiring bystanders that this hard-drinking gal with a penchant for pipe tobacco and men's breeches would become a Renaissance woman of crime.

She wasn't merely into misdemeanors, however. When Molly reached her forties, the British got into a hot and heavy civil war between the king and the Parliament. A rabid royal partisan, Molly took a hands-on part in the Great Rebellion, as it was called, by working as a highwayperson. In this capacity, on one famous occasion she whopped the daylights out of the commander-in-chief of the Parliamentary forces and his flunkies. After her first flush of patriotism, Ms. Cutpurse remembered she had a living to make—so she lightened the commander's load by 250 gold pieces. Moll got away clean; eventually, however, the livid commander caught her, and it was into the slammer. Not to worry, luv. Ever-thrifty Molly had enough put by to bribe her way to freedom, to the tune of 2,000 pounds.

When she'd had her fill of war and glory, Molly really got serious about her work, establishing a huge network of thieves. To handle the end results more efficiently, she set up a pawnshop business whose recycled contents were hotter than a Chernobyl backyard barbecue. When robbery turned humdrum, Moll would do a gig as a forger or a fortune-teller. Sometimes she would do a spell in Newgate—London's big prison. She didn't forget her friends in the joint, either, when she was out. On Sundays, Frith got into the habit of spending part of her ill-gotten gain on food for the prisoners. (In those days, English prisons allowed you to deliver.)

But a steady diet of crime makes anyone a dull delinquent, Moll believed. Her sexual escapades were numerous. Judging by her happy-go-lucky choice of partners, she may have been lesbian or bisexual. With her flair for the dramatic, Ms. Frith also plunged into the theater, supposedly becoming the first female to appear on the Elizabethan stage. In her role as a cavalier, she pretty much played herself—wore a doublet, sang a few off-color songs, that sort of thing. Already notorious, Moll became famous—especially when diverse enchanted Englishmen wrote several more songs and plays about the urban Robina Hood with the heart of gold.

In 1611, a comedy called "The Roaring Girle or Moll Cutpurse" opened at the Fortune stage in London. That same year, Moll herself got arrested in Saint Paul's cathedral for wearing men's duds—which goes to show that even a celebrity lowlife couldn't pursue her eccentricities in peace. But she kept trying: Moll lived to a strenuous seventy-five and would probably still be sending London bobbies up in smoke, if she hadn't dropped of the dropsy.

Phillipa of Hainault

ost medieval queens put in a good eight-hour day, doing everything from defending the castle to defending their honor from knights with more than courtly love on their minds.

The workweek of Queen Phillipa of Hainault easily went into overtime. From age nine, when an English bishop gave her the once-over for future queenhood, she knew where she was headed. Engaged to a twelve year old who in due time became Edward III of England, Phillipa eventually came to northern England from Flanders (now Belgium).

Besides her biological chores (royal heirs, of which she managed twelve), Phillipa was intensely interested in economics. As part of her marriage dowry loot, she'd gotten Norwich, known for its fine sheep and English wool. Her bright idea was to produce finished cloth, worth a great deal more than wool, both as an export and to clothe her scruffy-looking adoptive countrymen. To do so, she set up factories in Norwich and brought weavers and dyers from her home turf of Flanders to train local women. A monk later wrote about her, "Blessed be the name and memory of Queen Phillipa, who first invented English clothes."

No one-act economist, she followed up that success by founding England's other key industry: the coal operations at Tyndale. The queen was terrifically keen on higher learning, too. Besides endowing Queen's College at Oxford, she was patron to literary bigshots like Chaucer. She also busied herself with health care, founding several hospitals, and being both the angel and the patient of Cecilia, the most noted physician of Oxford.

Tall, golden-haired, and well-proportioned, Queen Phillipa had a wonderful maternal quality about her, which became legendary among the English—especially when, in an age of wet nurses, she personally breast-fed her gorgeous Gerber–baby boy Edward. She and Little Ed (later called the Black Prince for his flashy armor) became models for countless Madonna and child images, which can still be seen in English stained-glass windows and religious art.

Mom might not have looked the type to charge into battle, but she had opportunity to do that as well. In 1346, when Big Ed and Little Ed were busy scrapping elsewhere, some 12,000 Scots swarmed south to England with conquest on their minds. Queen Phillipa calmly stopped whatever else she was doing, donned armor, rallied the army, and made a "go get'em" speech from a white charger. In an afternoon, they had captured the Scots' king, David Bruce, and had his troops on the run. This derring-do tickled everyone; soon English gals everywhere packed jeweled daggers and wore hats shaped like helmets.

On occasion, the queen displayed that innate sense that enables women to get their way even when he's adamant. At Calais, for instance, when her husband had just clobbered the French and was preparing to behead half a dozen locals to serve as examples, who shows up but Phillipa—pregnant as usual. Knowing the king's press would be better if he showed a little mercy, Phillipa got on her knees and groveled for the locals' lives. Thanks to her clever submissiveness, Big Ed did the magnanimous thing and granted her favor.

The queen died in her fifties, much mourned; fortunately, she didn't have to witness the embarrassing hash that her widowed husband made of things, nor the early death of her beloved son, Little Ed.

Christine de Pizan

n 1365, Christine was still in diapers when her father got one of those can't-turn-down job offers from French King Charles V. The whole family moved from Venice to Paris; with Pop's prestigious new position as court astrologer, Christine got an Ivy League education. She was gonna need it, too.

At fifteen, she married a court notary named Estienne, and, as she later said, was supremely happy as wife and mother. But the plague hit, as it was wont to do in those days, and claimed Estienne. So there she was, a widow with two little kids, her mother, and her two brothers to support. Estienne hadn't left her squat. Neither had Chris' dad, whose astrology career and fortunes had gone into retrograde before he died. No largesse from the French king, either—although his librarian did allow Chris to keep on using his library.

As so many talented mothers with mouths to feed were to do after her, Christine turned her home into an office and became a working writer. Prolific from the start, she produced ten books of lyric poetry, eleven works of prose, satire, and the first important polemics on women's issues. No slouch at marketing, either, she managed to sell her second book to a duke for a sum that had other writers gnawing their knuckles in envy. After that, Pizan got commissions from a variety of patrons, royals mostly. Some of it was bread-and-butter work, like the official biography she wrote of Charles V.

The most enduring book she left may be *The Book of the City of Ladies,* a universal history of women, which exemplified what Pizan saw as the female affinity for learning. She also wrote a military manual; despite her much chuckled-over remarks that armies should be maintained only for defense, the book was widely popular and was even translated into English.

As her own book designer, she came to know the best illustrators (called "illuminators" then) in the business. Always eager to give other women a bump, Chris praised an illuminator with special talent named Anastasia, who obviously did some of the work on her books. (The subject of crediting had not yet become a touchy issue—at least to artists.)

Writing in Latin, and conversant in Italian and French also, Christine was unafraid to tackle the most controversial topic of her day: education and other rights for women. In her time, the gorgeously illustrated, sexy but highly sexist best-seller was *Romance of the Rose*—the "bible" for anyone with pretensions to courtly love. In 1403, Christine opened fire on its sexism with literary fireworks of her own, in a series of open letters to the author called a *querelle* (quarrel). Everybody who was anybody got copies of her challenging and highly political letters—which were later put into book format.

After a highly successful writing career that spanned twenty-nine years, Christine put down the pen and retired to a nunnery. She wrote only one more thing—but it was a dandy. In 1429, moved by the deeds of her gutsy sister *francaise*, Christine wrote a book to honor Joan of Arc. It was the only French book ever written about the Maid of Orleans in her lifetime.

Helene Kottanerin

New widowhood sounded pretty gloomy to Helene Kottanerin, a Hungarian with a hidden taste for derring-do. So around 1439, she remarried—this time to someone from the bright lights of Vienna who worked as a man-servant to cathedral bigwigs. His connections helped her win the post of lady-in-waiting to Queen Elizabeth of Hungary. "Lady in waiting" sounds seriously laidback: Helene was more like "lady in motion"—acting in rotation as the confidante, go-fer, and secret agent of Queen Lizzie.

One of her messier first chores was to assist at the birth of Queen Lizzie's son Ladislas, brand-new heir to the throne of Hungary and Bohemia. There was one complication; royal daddy, King Albert, had died unexpectedly three months prior—which meant the baby's chances of being declared king were slim-to-none. Having sized up Helene's abilities already, Queen Lizzie came up with a new assignment for her: whip on over to Visegrad Castle, where the royal crown was kept, liberate it, and bring it back to Lizzie and the infant, who would be holed up in a safe house out of the reach of the noble clique, who had their very own Polish candidate for the throne.

Helene rolled up her sleeves and set off on her mission improbable. The queen had neglected to mention a few trifling details: being mid-winter, snow and ice rendered travel difficult; the target castle was across the Danube River; and oh yes, if you get caught, you're on your own.

Some time later, in her tell-all memoir, Helene gleefully recounted the details of her heist. The toughest part came when she had to recross the frozen Danube with the grossly heavy goodies; her sled actually broke through the ice, and operative Kottanerin nearly became a Viennese ice sculpture.

Her fantastic feat a fact, the frostbitten lady-in-waiting laid the crown on baby and queen. A successful coup soon followed. Ironically, however, Queen Elizabeth died before the coup could really take hold, and Helene's horrendous efforts were all for nothing.

At that point, Helene could have updated her résumé, worked on her chillblains, or maybe joined her local "Forced to steal and commit other unspeakable crimes by the royal family" support group. Instead, she sat down and penned her autobiography. With the passage of time, the perspective it offers on a hidden slice of history has become more precious than any Hungarian crown—even though it remains to be translated into English.

Mission accomplished; why am I still lady-in-waiting for a reward?

Margaret of Scandinavia

ver hear about the Dane who united three Scandinavian countries in 1387 and ruled them as a union for twenty-five years? Margaret was her name; like several modern Margarets we could point to, she had a big brain, and she wasn't afraid to use it.

The first part of her life story was the usual marital-political alliance thing: Born a Danish princess, she married King Haakon of Norway and had a son, Olaf. When her father, the top dog of Denmark, died, Maggie began showing off her powers of persuasion. She cajoled the Danish Council into electing her five year old as king. Margaret would run the show behind the scenes as regent, she assured them. Five years after that ploy worked, she made the same pitch to the Norwegians. Sure, they said, and Margaret was now regenting two countries. (No mere on-paper alliance, either: This union between Norway and Denmark lasted for 400-plus years.)

There was a hitch when boy king, Olaf, got to be a teen—he died suddenly. Mastering her grief, this early Iron Maggie peacefully persuaded both Danes and Norwegians to forget the traditional order of succession and make her their ruler. Not being keen on women heads of state, the Danes decided to call her "sovereign lady, master, and guardian," while the Norwegians preferred the more casual sound of "mighty lady and master."

Within a month, the neighboring Swedes looked wistfully at her command of the situation, whimpered to get in, and hailed her as "sovereign lady and rightful master." Some of the more far-out Swedes in Lubeck actually called her "Lady King."

To make the Old Guard happy, Mighty Lady Number One shook her family tree for an obscure and conveniently young male relative who could be figurehead king on official letterhead. She came up with great-nephew Eric. Even after Eric was old enough to drink mead instead of milk, he and Margaret continued as a team. Eric worked the luncheon circuit and did the brewery grand openings, while she kept on with the actual work of governing, from developing a constitution for her "Scandinavia United We Stand" vision, to bringing Finland and Gotland into the fold.

This devoted Dane loved to organize. Day and night she worked on tax reform, monetary reform, developing a national assembly whose representatives came from both the townships and the nobility, and keeping bishops and other clergy from each others' throats. By the early 1400s, Margaret had pulled off the most horrendous task of all: melding the bureaucracy of three countries into one. To no one's shock, the Danish capital at Copenhagen became its capital city.

Her feats might not have seemed charismatic at the time, given the medieval tilt toward incessant warfare. Today, however, Maggie would probably get a Nobel peace prize for getting her Danes, Swedes, and Norwegians out of the German-based Hanseatic League, before it went down in economic and literal flames. When she died at fifty-nine, Margaret left an amazing legacy to Eric: a peaceful, prosperous Common Market of Scandinavia, as it were. Dismal news in Denmark—in spite of his long apprenticeship at the knees of Mighty Lady, Eric couldn't hold it together or produce an heir who could.

Juliana Berners

A very early environmentalist, English angler Juliana Berners understood the dangers of overfishing. As she wrote: "You must not be too greedy in catching your said game, as in taking too much at one time, a thing which can easily happen . . . our own sport and the other men's also."

Author of *The Boke of St. Albans,* which included the first treatise ever published on fly-fishing, Juliana was a prioress by trade, the head of Sopewell Nunnery in Saint Albans, England. In the off-season, it could get pretty quiet around the nunnery. Juliana, therefore, had a whole trout-string of justifications for dropping a line in the water: It made you get up early; It saved money; It promoted health. Fishing was soul food, she asserted: ". . . you will avoid idleness, which is the principal cause inciting many to other vices, as is right well-known."

This happy-go-lucky nature lover probably came from a titled family in Essex. Extremely well-educated, with a turn of phrase as delicate as her fly-casting, Juliana entered religious life but continued to love the outdoor pursuits of hunting, falconry, fowling, and fishing—and loved writing about them, too. For her book published in 1496, Juliana also made the illustrations of heraldic symbols and hand-calligraphed the text. Although its falconry chapters are fascinating, rod-and-reelers will get more out of *A Treatyse of Fysshynge Wyth an Angle,* whose how-to sections include making your own hooks and lines, tying flies, and the kind of fish lore that humans have been exchanging since time immemorial. A century after Juliana, a fellow fisherman and scribbler who admired her book sat down and wrote his own classic—Izaak Walton's *The Compleat Angler.*

Kuan Tao-sheng

While the Mongol hordes were busy conquering China in the mid-1200s, Kuan Tao-sheng was busy taking the country by storm with her bamboo paintings and her calligraphy. (Bamboo painting, a popular genre in Asian art, had been invented two centuries prior by Fu-jen, a female calligrapher with a bad case of insomnia. The story goes that one moonlit night, Fu-jen saw the eloquent shadows being made by the bamboo leaves outside, was reminded of work, got up and grabbed a calligraphy brush, and began to trace the shapes on her window. It helps to remember that Asians had windows made of rice paper.)

Blessed with a supportive husband, himself an artist and calligrapher, Kuan had a happy if mobile home life. The two had nine children together; they even collaborated artistically at times.

Husband Chao, who got his big break as court calligrapher for brand-new Mongol conqueror, Kublai Khan, soon got bumped upstairs. When he got promoted, the family moved from Peking to other parts of China, leading a corporate gypsy existence. Changing schools might have been hard on the kids, but, on the other hand, Kuan's visibility at court resulted in juicy commissions from the emperor—who was in an understandable hurry to shake his Mongol barbarian image and become a patron of culture. According to her husband's fond memoirs, Kuan received kudos on all sides and "imperial favors as abundant as rains." Some of that admiring downpour may even have come from a westerner named Marco Polo, who was a nearly permanent houseguest of the Kublai Khan. One of Kuan Tao-sheng's finest works, called *Bamboo Groves in Mist and Rain*, ended up in Taipei's National Palace Museum, where it can be marveled over today.

Marguerite of Navarra

An intellectual of Catholic tastes, Queen Marguerite got her kicks as a literary patron, mingling hard with everyone from Calvinist religious reformers to risqué French authors. When Rabelais dedicated his comedy *Gargantua and Pantagruel* to her, she was in heaven. How hard could it be to dash off wanton lines about the "brangle buttock-game," as Rabelais called it? Marguerite decided to try. To warm up, she wrote some religious poetry; despite its grabber title, *The Mirror of a Sinful Soul* got panned for its too-Lutheran tone. Then the queen coughed up what she thought was a real gem: *The Heptameron,* seventy-two tales with erotic themes—drawn from her life and her relatives. Trouble was, most of 'em hadn't done, said, or thought anything very arouse-worthy. Moreover, the queen made sure you got the moral of her stories by slamming them home with a two-by-four. (I guess Rabelais didn't run writers' workshops.) Fortunately, the queen included the true saga of Marguerite de la Roque in her collection—despite its sermonizing, that impudent pearl makes up for seventy-one empty oysters.

> *"Some there are who are much more ashamed of confessing a sin than of committing it."*

—from *The Heptameron*

Sukayna

ukayna, a cousin by marriage to Mohammed, didn't hesitate to drop the prophet's name in order to get the really hot singers, poets, and scholars to attend her lively gatherings of intellectual and musical give-and-take in her Arabian desert oasis. Not that she needed to cajole. Sizzling with brains and energy, Sukayna awakened other women to new standards of culture and education. Between all-night jam sessions and soirees, this early Moslem woman tied and untied the marital knot; the last go-around, she demanded—and got—complete freedom of action as part of the relationship. Her timing was superb, too. She had the fortune to live between 622 and 700, while the ideological and literal battles about the direction

Islam would take were still raging among Mohammed's many descendants. Soon thereafter, the Shi'ite sect of Islam came into being, whose fundamentalist precepts effectively shut the tent flaps on the likes of Sukayna and other women who had the gall to want freedom of speech, movement, and thought.

Properzia de' Rossi

Her dad was a paper-shuffler in fifteenth-century Bologna, but daughter Properzia thought that was a lot of baloney—she wanted to be an artist. As a teen, she studied drawing with local hot-shot engraver, Raimondi. Soon after, she made the city's must-see list of artists—or at least, artistic curiosities. Properzia got a kick out of carving; some people, however, couldn't resist calling her work "the pits." It seems this gimlet-eyed whittler recycled the stones from peaches, apricots, and even cherries for her miniature masterpieces. Besides decorating the Grassi family coat of arms with peach-stone apostles, Properzia even managed to carve complex scenes like the entire crucifixion onto a pit.

Once Properzia left her teens, she set about more serious work. She sculpted marble portrait busts, got a track record as a real artist, and then tapped into artistic paydirt: commissions.

One juicy assignment was a public grant to sculpt the high altar of a well-known church. Another break came when she won the bid in a prestigious local competition to create a number of marble sculptures for the church of San Petronio. She may not have signed her creations (few did in those days), but plenty of bureaucratic paperwork still exists to confirm Properzia's artistic output. At San Petronio, for instance, receipts indicate she got paid to sculpt two angels, three sibyls, and a couple of bas-relief panels in marble. Art historians are pretty sure that a panel depicting the Biblical story of *Joseph and Potiphar's Wife* is Properzia's work—and an eloquent seduction scene it is.

Like other women who chose to live the unconventional life of an artist, Properzia had to contend with jealous male competitors, vicious rumors about her sex life, vicious rumors about her nonexistent sex life, and other obstacles to happiness. Despite her apparent artistic and commercial successes, she most probably died in poverty before she was forty. This revolting conclusion might not seem too peachy to us, but perhaps the creative tradeoff was worth it for Properzia.

Alessandra Giliani

Renaissance women were famous for cutting remarks and glances; Alessandra Giliani of Bologna was famous for just plain cutting. This teenage prodigy got to study dissection at the side of the most famous slice-and-dice man in Italy, Mondino de Luzzi. In her time, around 1318, anatomy researchers weren't at all clear which blood vessels were veins and which were arteries. (This of course became horrifyingly important when someone had an arterial wound, for example.) Adroit Ales is credited with inventing a technique to trace the different blood vessels in the body. Using any cadaver handy, Alessandra would draw blood from the veins and arteries and refill them with different colored dyes that solidified, allowing anatomists to learn more about the human body. This science whiz was reputed to have died at nineteen, just plain drained by her labors. Today a plaque honoring her contribution to anatomy reposes in the Florence hospital church of Santa Maria del Mereto.

Rose of Burford

oaning money to a king is easy; the tricky bit is collecting, as Rose of Burford found out around 1320. Rose and her husband, John, worked in tandem as prominent London merchants in the wholesale wool business. As a member of a small group of merchants awarded the exclusive right to trade in a staple commodity, Rose exported English wool to the French across the channel.

Rose filled special orders, too. One came from Isabella of France, then queen, who commissioned a chic little cape adorned with coral as a gift for the current fashion-loving pope.

Rose had business acumen as sharp as a thorn. Not so hubby John, who also moonlighted as the sheriff of London. Maybe he suffered from sleep deprivation; in any event, John definitely carried the "currying royal favor" policy too far when he fronted King Edward II a substantial sum to tide him over in his war against the Scots. You know how wars are—cost overruns, always.

Shortly thereafter, John died. Among other things, the new widow found to her dismay that good ole King Eddie hadn't paid back the loan. Did our English rose keep a stiff upper lip and write the king off in the "bad debts" column? Not on your life: Being executor of John's will, Rose felt obliged to go after the assets of the estate—even if it meant ticking off the royals.

Documents still kicking around from her day show that she petitioned the king at least five times, to no avail. So what do you do in the touchy event that the Big Stilton of England refuses to answer petitions? Our gutsy wool merchant followed through by providing King Eddie with a solution of her own devising. Since Rose had to pay taxes on her own wool and skins for export, she suggested running a tab of her duties payable and debiting them against the king's loan. This lucid proposal was an immediate hit with the uncreditworthy monarch, who said, "Make it so."

Rose got repaid, and a good thing too; a few years later, she got into debt herself—and found her own goods confiscated in the port of Dover to repay the debt. (Need I add that neither King Eddie nor anyone else jumped in with advice, cash, or credit?)

Chu Shu-chen

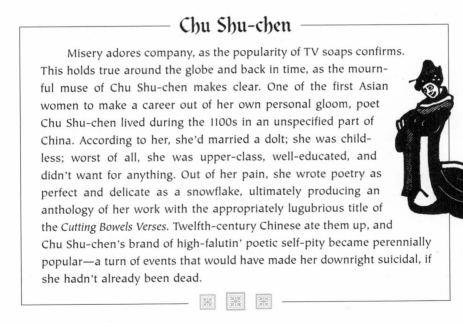

Misery adores company, as the popularity of TV soaps confirms. This holds true around the globe and back in time, as the mournful muse of Chu Shu-chen makes clear. One of the first Asian women to make a career out of her own personal gloom, poet Chu Shu-chen lived during the 1100s in an unspecified part of China. According to her, she'd married a dolt; she was childless; worst of all, she was upper-class, well-educated, and didn't want for anything. Out of her pain, she wrote poetry as perfect and delicate as a snowflake, ultimately producing an anthology of her work with the appropriately lugubrious title of the *Cutting Bowels Verses*. Twelfth-century Chinese ate them up, and Chu Shu-chen's brand of high-falutin' poetic self-pity became perennially popular—a turn of events that would have made her downright suicidal, if she hadn't already been dead.

Queen Elizabeth the First

etween 1533 and 1603, the English didn't need television. Watching the life of their Number One Elizabethan held more than enough fascination. The quirky personality of Elizabeth Tudor, with her perilous childhood, her does-she, doesn't-she love life, the political pickles she got into and out of, was made for syndication. Above all else, she had royal presence. From her father, Henry VIII, she got theatrical gold-red hair, skin as pale and translucent as 2 percent low-fat, and long bejeweled fingers. From the ghastly fates of her mother, Anne Boleyn, and her stepmother Catherine, both beheaded before her eighth birthday, Elizabeth received her determination to stay independent. Date, flirt, string along, you bet. Marry? Never.

When she became queen, a council memo of the day took note of the status quo: "... the realm is exhausted, the people out of order, steadfast enemies, but no steadfast friends ..." In her reign, Elizabeth brought about prosperity (it took her fifteen years just to pay off the debts left by her father); peace (besides ending the war with France, she whipped the Spanish Armada); and a golden age of literature, drama, and the arts. Not too shabby for a career virgin who was reputed to be bald at thirty.

The virginity and baldness issues both need an update. Although Elizabeth did catch smallpox, it didn't cause permanent hair loss. In fact, a devoted friend named Mary Sidney nursed her through it—and was horribly disfigured when *she* got a severe case. The "bald queen" thing seems to stem from Liz' love of wigs—and a series of male historians who lazily passed the tale along. When the queen thought herself at death's door with smallpox, she rattled off a bequest to "Sweet Robin," aka

Lord Robert Dudley, love of her life and her suitor for years. At the same time, she willed quite a sum of money to his man-servant, who would have witnessed their intimacies. Clinically speaking, it sounds like the queen engaged in a variety of sexual activities, but not the main event.

A royal of pronounced likes and dislikes, this tall Tudor adored fresh flowers, fireworks, the theater, vanilla (she put it on everything), pearls, silk stockings, archery, fantastical clothes, vigorous dancing, bathing, and the colors white, black, gold, and ginger. Unlike other Elizabethans, she hated unwashed bodies and bad smells. In 1597, her godson got on her good side forever when he invented and installed a water closet for her. Liz exhibited plenty of contradictions, too. Although she called the enslavement of Africans detestable, she lent one of her ships to a profitable slave-running venture. She loathed the royal habit of keeping dwarfs at court—yet she had one of her own, a diminutive lady named Mrs. Tomasin.

Near the end of her forty-five-year reign, Good Queen Bess said: "Though God has raised me high, yet this I count the glory of my crown that I have reigned with your loves. I do not so much rejoice that God has made me a Queen, as to be a Queen over so thankful a people." That love was amply reciprocated. Seldom has a leader been as well-loved and as competent at being a ruler as this queen who gave her name to an entire era.

Beatrix Galindo

The fifteenth century was one of those times when higher education for women had a priority of zilch; in fact, the only country to which women with a yen for a degree could go was Italy. The university at Salerno, Italy, long famous for its list of overachieving women, also was alma mater to Spaniard Beatrix Galindo. When she had sheepskin in hand, Galindo made a beeline back to Spain, where she nabbed a post as professor of Latin and philosophy at the super-prestigious University of Salamanca. Nicknamed "La Latina" for her command of that language, brainy Bea came to the attention of Queen Isabel, who hired her for private lessons at the Spanish court. With Bea's help, royal daughter Juana also got good enough at Latin to make impromptu speeches (not that she was allowed to make many). Teaching, however, failed to meet the intellectual challenge for the likes of Galindo, who lived to be sixty and filled in her idle hours by founding a hospital in Madrid.

BIBLIOGRAPHY

A surprising amount of creative output—writings, music, and art—by medieval women survives. Much research continues to be done on women of this period also, often published by university presses. Boldfaced items contain works of or excerpts by the uppity women profiled in this book.

Amt, Emilie, ed. **Women's Lives in Medieval Europe.** Routledge Chapman, 1993.

Barber, Elizabeth *Women's Work: the First 20,000 Years.* Norton, 1994.

Barnstone, Willis. **A Book of Women Poets.** Harper & Row, 1980.

Barstow, Anne. *Witchcraze.* HarperCollins, 1994.

Berners, Dame Juliana. **The Boke of Saint Albans.** Da Capo Press, 1969.

Bogin, Meg. **The Women Troubadours.** Norton, 1980.

Boulding, Elise. *The Underside of History.* Sage Publications, 1992.

Brazell, Karen. **The Confessions of Lady Nijo.** Stanford University Press, 1973.

Brown, Judith. **Immodest Acts—the Life of a Lesbian Nun in Renaissance Italy.** Oxford University Press, 1986.

Bynum, Caroline. *Holy Feast and Holy Fast.* University of California Press, 1987.

Collis, Louise. **Memoirs of a Medieval Woman—the Life and Times of Margery Kempe.** Harper & Row, 1964.

Comnena, Anna. **The Alexiad.** Penguin, 1969.

Cross, Donna. *Pope Joan.* Crown, 1996.

Davis, N., ed. **Paston Letters.** Clarendon Press, 1958.

Diaz del Castillo, Bernal. *The Discovery and Conquest of Mexico.* Farrar Straus & Giroux, 1956.

Eisler, Riane. *The Chalice and the Blade: Our History, Our Future.* Harper & Row, 1987.

_____. *Sacred Pleasure: Sex, Myth, and the Politics of the Body.* HarperCollins, 1995.

Ellis, Peter. *Celtic Women.* Eerdsman Publishing, 1996.

Erauso, Catalina de. *Lieutenant Nun: Memoir of a Basque Transvestite in the New World.* Beacon, 1996.

Fraser, Antonia. *Warrior Queens.* Vintage, 1990.

Gabrieli, Francesco. *Arab Historians of the Crusades.* University of California Press, 1969.

Gies, Frances and Joseph. *Women in the Middle Ages.* Crowell, 1978.

_____. *Life in a Medieval City.* Crowell, 1969.

Harksen, Sibylle. *Women in the Middle Ages.* Schram, 1975.

Hauser, Ernest. *Italy, a Cultural Guide.* Atheneum, 1981.

Heller, Nancy. *Women Artists, an Illustrated History.* Abbeville, 1987.

Heloise. *The Letters of Abelard and Heloise.* Penguin, 1974.

Henry, Sondra, & Taitz, Emily. *Written out of History: Jewish Foremothers.* Biblio Press, 1990.

Herlihy, David. *Opera Muliebra: Women and Work in Medieval Europe.* McGraw-Hill, 1990.

Hildegard of Bingen. *Illuminations.* Bear Publishing, 1985.

Karlen, Arno. *Man and Microbes.* Putnam, 1995.

Kempe, Margery. *The Book of Margery Kempe.* Oxford University Press, 1940.

King, Margaret. *Women of the Renaissance.* University of Chicago Press, 1991.

Labarge, Margaret. *A Small Sound of the Trumpet.* Beacon Press, 1986.

Larrington, Carolyne. *Women and Writing in Medieval Europe.* Routledge, 1995.

Macksey, Joan, et al. *Guinness Book of Women's Achievements.* Stein and Day, 1975.

Minai, Naila. *Women in Islam.* Seaview Books, 1981.

Morison, Samuel. *The Great Explorers.* Oxford University Press, 1978.

Oglivie, Marilyn. *Women in Science: Antiquity Through the 19th Century.* MIT Press, 1993.

Pizan, Christine. *The Book of the City of Ladies.* Persea, 1982.

Power, Eileen. *Medieval Women.* Cambridge University Press, 1975.

Procopius. *Secret History.* University of Michigan Press, 1966.

Raven, Susan, et al. *Women of Achievement.* Harmony Books, 1981.

Rosenthal, Joel, ed. *Medieval Women and the Sources of Medieval History.* University of Georgia Press, 1990.

Roth, Cecil. *The House of Nasi—Doña Gracia.* Jewish Publishing Society, 1948.

Salmonson, Jessica. *The Encyclopedia of Amazons.* Doubleday, 1991.

Thomas, Hugh. *Conquest: Montezuma, Cortes, and the Fall of Old Mexico.* Simon & Schuster, 1993.

Trager, James. *The Women's Chronology.* Holt, 1994.

Uitz, Erika. *The Legend of Good Women.* Moyer Bell, 1994.

Walker, Barbara. *Woman's Encyclopedia of Myths and Secrets.* Harper & Row, 1983.

Wiesner, Merry. *Working Women in Renaissance Germany.* Rutgers University Press, 1986.

RECOMMENDED MUSIC, VIDEO:

Hildegard. Vision: *The Music of Hildegard von Bingen,* Angel Records.

_____. *Canticles of Ecstacy,* BMG Music.

Trobaritz (female troubadours). *"The sweet look and the loving manner,"* Sinfonye, Hyperion.

Juana la Loca. *Music for Joan the Mad, La Nef,* Dorian Discovery.

The Crusades: 3-part video series; Terry Jones. New Video Group 1995.

INDEX

For space reasons, this alphabetical index lists only female names. Some of these women had no surnames; others had a secondary geographic or work-related name; still others had three or four monikers. Therefore, this index is alphabetized by first name. Even where available, birth/death dates are argued over. Where unavailable, entries are labeled "a." (when active) and/or "c." (about).

Because literacy was low, printing new-fangled, and spelling standardization non-existent, medieval women's names had numerous variations. For sanity's sake, we've used one version, and stuck with it.

ACKNOWLEDGMENTS

A special thanks to those who pointed me toward women, events, information, and insights I might not otherwise have found:

Meg Bogin; Sara Bodlak; Serim Denel; Riane Eisler; Denise Fourie; Doris Gold, editor of Biblio Press; Joni Hunt; Terry Jones; Barbara Lane; Ed Landry; Pamela Lechtman; Penny Lentz; the Lyon(s) Families Association of America; Emily McGinn; Karen Mellin; Ginny and Paul Merz; Paula Ogren; Harry Ojalvo, Curator of the Quincentennial Foundation in Istanbul; Oxford University Press; Lissi Pedley; Shirley Ranck; Michael Shulman of Archive Photos; Judith Steinmetz; Nedim Yahya of the Quincentennial Foundation.

Vicki León

The author of over twenty books, including *Uppity Women of Ancient Times*, Vicki León also delights in giving workshops and speeches on the unsung women of history. She lives in Southern California.

Talk about history coming to life—while researching this book, author León discovered a woman who may be her earliest known medieval ancestor—Adelicia Louvein.

✿ ✿ ✿ ✿ ✿ ✿ ✿

Adelicia Louvein

It all started in 1120, when Adelicia, a French duke's daughter so delicious she was called "the Fair Maid of Brabant," got the nod to become the second wife of King Henry the First of England. This was no piece-a-cake assignment—the man's only hobby was siring kids out of wedlock. Adelicia also inherited Matilda, a feisty stepdaughter her own age. When the Fair Maid wed Henry, he'd just lost his only legitimate son—but the gloom around the Castle of Lyons *really* thickened as the years rolled by and Adelicia failed to get pregnant. The queen kept an upbeat attitude, becoming pals with her stepdaughter; the king never lightened up. Maybe his problem was acid indigestion, not sorrow; in 1133, he expired after eating one too many lamprey eels. Adelicia then fell in love and wed a knight nicknamed "Strong Arm." Living in Arundel Castle near the Sussex coast, they were happily growing a family of seven when Matilda landed on the doorstep. She'd been named queen by Henry, who made everyone swear allegiance. Lot of good that did; she'd been in battle ever since. Her main rival now insisted that Adelicia surrender Matilda to him. With only a skeleton crew to defend her castle, the Fair Maid was not in a good bargaining position. Nevertheless, she boldly told the rival to buzz off, saying that she'd protect her stepdaughter to the last extremity. Her bluff worked—for the moment. Years of war later, the steady support of Adelicia and husband would help Matilda's son become King Henry the Second, the first ruler of England's most beloved dynasty—the Plantagenets. Adelicia remains a shining memory for her descendants, now a worldwide pride of Lyons, Linnes, and Leóns.

Wild Women Association

In 1992, with the publication of *Wild Women* by Autumn Stephens, Conari Press founded the Wild Women Association. Today there are over 3,000 card-carrying Wild Women in cities throughout the world—and some even meet regularly with their untamed (and often uproarious) sisters in an effort to encourage brazen behavior. The Association's primary purpose is to rediscover and write our fabulously unruly foremothers back into history. . . . and if there is a wild woman in your family we hope you might help by sending us information for possible inclusion in subsequent volumes of the Wild Women series.

To become a member and to receive the Wild Women Association Newsletter, please mail this page to:

The Wild Women Association
2550 Ninth Street, Suite 101
Berkeley, CA 94710

Let's rewrite history with women in it!

Other Books in the
Uppity and ever so **Wild** Women series:

Uppity Women of Ancient Times
by Vicki León

Wild Women
*Crusaders, Curmudgeons and Completely Corsetless Ladies
in the Otherwise Virtuous Victorian Era*
by Autumn Stephens

Wild Women in the White House
*The formidable Females Behind the Throne,
On the phone, and (Sometimes) Under the Bed*
by Autumn Stephens

Wild Women in the Kitchen
*101 Rambunctious Recipes &
99 Tasty Tales*
by The Wild Women Association

Wild Words from Wild Women
*An Unbridled Collection of Candid Observations
& Extremely Opinionated Bon Mots*
by Autumn Stephens

Conari Press, established in 1987, publishes books on topics
ranging from spirituality and women's history to sexuality and
personal growth. Our main goal is to publish quality books
that will make a difference in people's lives—both
how we feel about ourselves and how
we relate to one another.

Our readers are our most important resource, and we
value your input, suggestions, and ideas. We'd love to hear
from you—after all, we are publishing
books for you!

*For a complete catalog or to get on our mailing list,
please contact us at:*

CONARI PRESS
2550 Ninth Street, Suite 101
Berkeley, CA 94710

800 • 685 • 9595   Fax 510 • 649 • 7190
e-mail: conaripub@aol.com